ADVANCE PRA~

"With *Gilded Girls* Chartier and Enss have again shown us an overlooked facet of the women of the Old West. . . . A must-read for anyone who wants a well-rounded knowledge of the 1800s in western America."

—Dakota and Sunny Livesay, *Chronicle of the Old West* newspaper

"*Gilded Girls* is a delicious, illuminating glimpse at the colorful and often scandalous women who made their living performing for the restless souls of the Old West."

—Bob Boze Bell, *True West* magazine

"*Gilded Girls* presents a fascinating array of extraordinary, gutsy women who forged legacies as unforgettable entertainers for the restless souls of the Old West."

—Sheri Brummond, Rosemont Film Productions

"Before the hottest performer today, the unforgettable, feisty women in the Old West saga *Gilded Girls* reigned supreme as the most luscious kind of talent available—truly a wonderful, scathing read!"

—Jennie Lew Tugend, Capstone Pictures

Gilded Girls

Women Entertainers of the Old West

JoeAnn Chartier

Chris Enss

TWODOT®

GUILFORD, CONNECTICUT
HELENA, MONTANA
AN IMPRINT OF THE GLOBE PEQUOT PRESS

A · TWODOT® · BOOK

TwoDot is a registered trademark of The Globe Pequot Press.

Cover photos: frame courtesy Image Club; portrait of Kate Rockwell courtesy Barrett Willoughby, Alaska and Polar Regions Archives, Rasmuson Library, University of Alaska Fairbanks

Text design: Lisa Reneson

The Will Rogers newspaper quote on page 125 was reprinted with permission from the Will Rogers Memorial in Claremore, Oklahoma.

Library of Congress Cataloging-in-Publication Data
Enss, Chris.
    Gilded girls : women entertainers of the old West / Chris Enss and JoAnn Chartier.—1st ed.
        p. cm.
    Includes biographical references and index.
    ISBN 0-7627-2679-2
        I. Women entertainers—West (U.S.)—Biography. I. Chartier, JoAnn. II. Title.

PN2286.8.E57 2003
791'.092'278—dc21   2003048053

Manufactured in the United States of America
First Edition/Third Printing

To all my extended family for the laugh lines you've given me

—J.C.

For the first entertaining ladies in my life, my mother, grandmother, and Aunt Darla

—C.E.

Contents

Acknowledgments

We are indebted to the many people who helped in assembling material for this book. We wish to acknowledge with gratitude Jim Ricker of the Oklahoma Territorial Museum for information and records pertaining to Lucille Mulhall; Lisa Lehman at the Rasmuson Library, University of Alaska, for supplying material for the chapter on Kate Rockwell; the fine staff at the California State Library for helping to gather information on many of the talented entertainers contained in this publication; the knowledgeable and indulgent personnel at the Searl's and Nevada County Historical Libraries; Mrs. Lee Cox at the San Francisco Performing Arts Library and Museum for locating Dr. Robinson's songs and plays; librarian Michael Maher, staff, and volunteers at the Nevada Historical Society in Reno; Kathy Hodges for her assistance with five boxes of theater materials at the Idaho Historical Society Library and Archives in Boise; the staff at the Butte–Silver Bow Archives in Montana; and, finally, Carol Anderson at the Nevada County Library for arranging inter-library loans and obtaining copies of obscure source materials.

A special thank-you to fine editors Himeka Curiel and Justine Rathbun for their professional expertise, and to Charlene Patterson for seeing this work through the process.

Introduction

A new phase is coming over theatricals in California. Nothing will do now but stars; and even they must be of the first magnitude. The Californians are as good judges of acting as can be found anywhere; and they care not a fig for the opinion of New York or London. When we pronounce a favorable verdict, we are able to back it up with a fortune, and snap our fingers in the face of the world.

—The *Pioneer* magazine, San Francisco, 1854

In 1847 the western territory of the United States was a sleepy wilderness populated mostly by Indians and Mexicans. But when word reached the eastern states that there were rich deposits of gold in the mountains of the frontier, the region changed virtually overnight. Two hundred thousand restless souls, mostly men, but including some women and children, traveled to the untamed western lands, primarily to California, during the first three years of the Gold Rush. They came from all over the world, leaving homes and families for the dream of finding riches.

Soon the West was dotted with mining boomtowns and bustling new cities. Fortunes were made and lost daily. Lawlessness was commonplace. At first gold seekers were content with the crude entertainment provided by ragtag bands and their own amateur fiddle-playing neighbors. They flocked to bear-wrestling and prize-fighting exhibitions. In this impetuous atmosphere gambling dens, saloons, brothels, and dance halls thrived, but after a while, the miners and merchants began to long for more polished amusements. Theaters, backstreet halls, tents, palladiums, auditoriums, and jewel-box-sized playhouses went up quickly and stayed busy, their thin walls resounding with operas, arias, verses from Shakespeare, and minstrel tunes.

The western pioneers' passion for diversion lured brave actors, dancers, singers, and daredevils west. Entertainers endured the same primitive conditions as other newcomers. They lived in tents and deserted ships and canvas houses or paid enormous rents for the few available wooden cabins. But nineteenth-century thespians were often prepared for such a lifestyle. Acting was largely an itinerant profession at the time, and most players earned their living barnstorming from town to town and even from country to country, performing different plays or musical numbers from a large repertoire every night of the week. Bored miners were willing to pay high sums to these entertainers, especially to the females.

Many of the most popular women entertainers of the mid- and late-1800s performed in the boomtowns that dotted the West, drawn by the same desires for riches and bringing a variety of talents and programs. They were mostly well received and sometimes literally showered with gold, but their personal lives were often marked by tragedy and unhappiness. Within the chapters of this book are the stories of a few of these gifted thespians who brought glitz, glamour, and genius to western America. The footlights have been illuminated, and the curtain is about to go up, revealing the tales of fourteen women entertainers who captured the hearts of the western pioneers.

Maude Adams

THE MOST POPULAR ACTRESS IN AMERICA

I wish you could have seen Maudie that night. She was simply wriggling with excitement. It was all I could do to keep her in her dressing-room until the cue came for her to go on. . . . Just before the curtain went up I made her repeat her first-act lines to me. She had learned them like a parrot, to be sure, but she spoke them like a true little actress.

—Annie Adams's comments about her daughter Maude's
performance at the age of five at the Metropolitan Theater in San Francisco

The Palmer Theater House in New York was jammed to the doors by curious clientele, all there to see the new actress, Maude Adams, play opposite the most celebrated actor of the day, John Drew. It was October 3, 1892, when the stunning, elfin Maude Adams took the stage in the play *The Masked Ball*. Although Drew was congratulated on his admirable acting job, by the end of the evening Maude had scored a hit that was bigger than his entire career. The applause, which lasted for a full two minutes after her exit, indicated she was on her way to becoming a star. Local newspapers predicted her talent would be talked about for years to come. As the *New York Daily News* reported:

> Her performance was a revelation. There is one scene in the
> second act where in order to punish her husband for some
> antenuptial remarks of his she has to pretend that she is
> drunk. It was just touch and go whether the scene ruined the

3

MAUDE ADAMS 1872–1953

play or not. It would have been hard to devise a more crucial test for an actress of even the wildest experience and the greatest skill. In order to carry off this scene successfully it was necessary for the wife to appear to be drunk and yet be a gentlewoman at the same time. Miss Adams achieved this feat. If Miss Adams had done nothing else throughout the entire play than that one scene it would have stamped her as a comedienne of the first order forever.

Maude Adams's stage career began at the tender age of nine months. The play was called *The Lost Child*, and the baby that was playing the title character became fussy and could not continue in the show after the first act. Maude's mother, Annie, who was the female lead in the production, suggested her daughter take the child's place. Maude was so good that the other baby received two weeks' notice immediately after the play ended. For the remainder of that season, all the infant roles in the plays done by Annie's company were played by little Miss Maude.

Maude Ewing Adams Kiskadden was born on November 1, 1872, in Salt Lake City. Her mother was a leading lady in the stock company that played the local social hall. Her father, James Kiskadden, worked for a bank and in the mines. Although Maude was quite a success as a baby actress, James was reluctant to let his daughter become a professional performer. "She's my only daughter," he told his wife, "and I've no intention of letting her go on the stage and make a fool of herself." At five years of age, Maude informed her father that she would like to go on the stage and promised that she would not make a fool of herself. James reluctantly gave in to the child's request.

Maude's first acting role, when she was five years old, was the character of Little Schneider in the play *Fritz*. She had nearly one hundred lines to speak in the play, and she memorized them all in a couple of days. Critics hailed her first-night performance as letter perfect. The theater managers were so impressed with her talents that they began to note her on the program as "Little Maudie," and it was by that name that she was known in the West throughout her career as a child actress.

By the age of seven, Little Maudie was the reigning child actress of the Pacific Slope. David Belasco, known as the greatest American stage manager of all time, became the child star's manager. He was captivated by her talent and charm, and along with Annie he shaped Maude into the acting legacy she became. In his memoirs he wrote of his first meeting with Maude:

> There was a magnetism about the child, traces even then of that wonderfully sweet and charming personality which was to prove such a tremendous advantage to her in the later years. The child, in short, was a born artist: she had temperament. She could act and grasp the meaning of a part long before she was able to read. When we were beginning rehearsals of a new play I would take Maudie on my knee and bit by bit would explain to her the meaning of the part she had to play. I can see her now, with her little spindle legs almost touching the floor, her tiny face, none too clean, perhaps, peering into mine, and those wise eyes of hers drinking in every word.
>
> I soon learned that it was no use to confine myself to a description of her own work: until I had told the whole story of the play to Maudie, and treated her almost as seriously as if she were our leading star, she would pay no attention. She was serious minded in her own childish way even in those days, and once she realized that you were treating her seriously there was nothing that that child would not try to do.

Annie doted on her child and was immensely proud of her acting ability. She learned Maude's parts as well as her own. Everywhere the mother and daughter team went they practiced their lines together, and Annie helped her daughter understand each character she was to portray. They practiced in their dressing rooms, on the street cars, and at home. Maude had an exceptional memory and was a quick study. David was inspired by Annie's attention to her daughter's career and years later recalled how he could never see the child on stage without a picture rising up before him of her hardworking, self-sacrificing mother:

> Stage people, with all their faults, are probably the warmest-hearted in the world, but never in all my long experience have I seen an instance of such unselfish, idolizing devotion as Mrs. Adams displayed for her little girl. Of course it's the most natural thing in the world for any mother to love her child, but Mrs. Adams' love was something quite out of the common.

David Belasco's management skills combined with Annie Adams's tutelage helped make Maude Adams one of the most successful child stars in the West, but a couple of quick growth spurts made it impossible for her to continue playing children's parts any longer. She turned ten in 1882, and her mother decided Maude needed to temporarily retire from the theater in order to attend school. She enrolled her in the Presbyterian Collegiate Institute in Salt Lake City, where, for four years, Maude studied drama and all matters of theatrical production. She also became proficient at the harp and learned to speak French fluently.

Maude missed her mother terribly during her years at the institute. She missed her home and the stage as well. She wrote Annie, begging her to let her return to her "old work." "It's no use my studying anymore, Mother," Maude continued. "In fact it's all nonsense unless I'm to go into literature or am to be a teacher. But I want to go on the stage again, so that I may be with you."

After four years, Annie gave in to her daughter's urgings and allowed Maude to come home. The stage life she had left, however, was not waiting anxiously for her to return. Her accomplishments as a child actress were mostly forgotten. She

Because of her youthful appearance, Maude often played young characters. J. M. Barrie said that he wrote the role of Peter Pan, the boy who never grew up, especially for Maude.

found herself as a mere nonentity: Annie Adams's daughter. Nevertheless she was able to take parts as an extra, and she gave one hundred percent even in those small roles.

Annie decided to take the teenager to New York, where theatrical parts were abundant and where Maude might be offered more challenging roles. After auditioning for several shows, Maude landed a role in the play *The Paymaster*. For the first time she was billed on the program as Maude Adams, rather than "Little Maudie" as she had been known in the beginning. David Belasco was in the audience the night the play opened. Although he hadn't seen Maude for seven years, he was struck by her performance:

> Her part in the play was rather an important one, and I saw at once that there was the making of a charming actress in her. If I remember right, Charles Frohman [another stage manager] saw her in this same performance and felt as I did. At all events, some time later, when he was organizing a stock company, we both thought of her for one of the ingénues. But then, that wasn't so much credit to us, either, for by that time Miss Adams had already been discovered and engaged by Charles Hoyt, and had played with great success at the Bijou in *A Midnight Bell*.

At the end of the run of *A Midnight Bell*, Maude was a much-talked-about actress. In all parts of town, people were asking one another if they "had seen the new little girl in Hoyt's play at the Bijou." Everyone agreed that she was sweet and talented. Offers began pouring in for Maude to star in various productions around town. Charles Hoyt, a prominent theatrical manager, was willing to let her name her own terms if she would sign a five-year contract with him, as he knew he would strike gold with her talent. He offered her lead roles in a series of comedies, but Maude declined and signed with manager Charles Frohman. She had decided she wanted to focus on doing serious dramas, and Frohman promised her the opportunity.

Frohman hired professional playwrights to create roles for Maude that would give her the chance to exercise her talent to the fullest. The first result was Nell, the lame girl, in a play called *The Lost Paradise*. It was a charming role that showed for the first time what Maude could do in the way of pathos. The favorable reviews led Charles to team the actress with the most popular actor of the day, John Drew. It was a stroke of management genius, one that would launch Maude as one of the most popular American actresses in the world. Critics and audiences alike raved about her performances and flocked to the theater to see her every chance they got.

John Drew and Maude Adams worked together in six different plays. Newspaper reviewers wrote that "she arrived on the other side of her teaming up with Drew as one of the most accomplished and womanly artists of all the younger actresses." At this point Frohman decided the time was ripe for Maude to come out as a star in a larger venue.

Charles Frohman searched for a vehicle that would secure her in this position. He hired the well-known Scottish author J. M. Barrie (author of *Peter Pan*) to turn his popular novel *The Little Minister* into a play. Barrie delivered a powerful manuscript, which both Frohman and Maude agreed would make for a stellar debut. Miss Adams made her first metropolitan appearance at the Empire Theater in New York on September 28, 1897. The play was a huge success, a success in which Maude Adams as an artist and J. M. Barrie as a playwright shared almost equally.

The *New York Daily News* wrote:

> Rarely has a star been born under more auspicious circumstances. Miss Adams threw her whole soul into her work in this role. And well she might, for Lady Babbie was a part after her own heart. She is simply a little devil who loves a joke even more than she loves her lover, but playwright Barrie had contrived two or three serious little scenes in the midst of the fun, which shows that after all the Lady Babbie

is deeper than she seems and Maude Adams more talented that we realized.

Maude took her Lady Babbie role west in 1898. Sunday schools cried for her and clergymen of all denominations flocked to see *The Little Minister*. From coast to coast the verdict seemed universal: The only thing better than the play was Maude Adams herself. Her popularity soared. Clever businessmen cashed in on that popularity, naming products they sold or manufactured, from children's toys to corsets to cigars, after the star.

Maude, however, was uneasy with her newfound fame. She was pleased with the attention but fearful that audiences would never accept her in any role other than Lady Babbie. She decided to study Shakespeare and soon had mastered the role of Juliet. Seeing her drive and dedication, Frohman hired a special company of actors and produced *Romeo and Juliet*. By May 1898 Maude's interpretation of Juliet had been seen in all the leading cities in America. She deviated from the traditional presentation of the character by playing Juliet as a simple, girlish creature with infinite charm. Her performance was recognized by the masses as being "the master-stroke of a very clever woman." Maude now looked upon her career with a renewed sense of confidence, having proven to herself that audiences appreciated her talent regardless of the part she was playing.

Maude followed up her performance in *Romeo and Juliet* with lead roles in the plays *L'Aiglon*, *Quality Street*, and *Joan of Arc*. In between shows she returned to Utah to visit her family. She spent a lot of time with her grandmother, inspired by their conversations and the lovely valley of the Salt Lake. "At grandmother's house," she later told an interviewer with Salt Lake City's *Desert News Centennial* newspaper, "there were vastly entertaining things: cows and sheep and horses and dogs. And trees to climb with cherries at the top. And oh, the sweet-smelling hay in the barn and the swing tied to one of the rafters. There were fields to roam, whole fields of wild flowers—freedom."

Very little is known about Maude's personal life. She was intensely private and took great pride in the fact that there was scarcely a woman onstage that the public knew less about. Historians record that she loved horses and was an exceptional rider. She owned a homestead and farm on Long Island. In the early 1900s she suffered a nervous breakdown from overwork on the stage. It is rumored that she was deeply in love with her mentor and manager, Charles Frohman, but since she drew the line very distinctly between her stage career and her private life, little can be substantiated in regard to any affair between the two.

In an interview for a national magazine in 1894, Maude commented on her reasons for not wanting to share her personal life: "I don't see why an actress must give her personality to the world, though it seems to be expected, and those who curiously investigate her personal life are not always careful how they use their information."

In 1904 Maude starred as Peter Pan in one of the most enduring and beloved children's plays ever written. J. M. Barrie adapted the part especially for her and conveyed in a letter to the actress that she had inspired the character of the boy who refused to grow up. Maude performed the role in more than 1,500 performances. During the play's run she never left the theater if there was a chance children would be waiting outside because she didn't want to spoil their illusion of the magical flying boy by letting them see her as a woman. When she played the role in Salt Lake City, children from local orphanages attended the matinee. The director of St. Ann's Orphanage later said, "The only trouble is that it has kept the entire corps of nurses busy trying to prevent the children from flying out the windows."

Maude followed up her success as Peter Pan with starring roles in three more Barrie plays: *The Pretty Sister of Jose*, *The Jesters*, and *What Every Woman Knows*. Outside the Metropolitan Theater in San Francisco, one of her favorite western venues, was the Hearst Greek Theater of the University of California at Berkeley. There she introduced audiences to a variety of intriguing characters created by Edmond Rostand. Audiences consistently called her performances "remarkable."

Maude's accomplishments as a thespian were exceptional, but she excelled in the art of stage lighting as well. She had always been fascinated with the technical aspects of putting on a show. Gifted actor Lionel Barrymore remarked in his auto-biography that Maude "could not resist supervising the lights for any given per-formance." She felt proper lighting could enhance an actor's onstage presence. "What color to use in footlights," she told the *Desert New Centennial,* "was always a matter for discussion. On those afternoons, in the great, quiet theater, all the colors of the rainbow would dance up and down for our information and delight. A strug-gle was going on with a series of blue footlights for night scenes; blue demanded a special makeup which allowed no pink cheeks. That was a bother, for when the white lights were turned on, a heroine with ghastly white cheeks was not exactly attractive."

With the help of a skilled electrician, Maude created the widely used dimmer box, a main switchboard that controls every light used in the production of a show, including the spotlights. In 1921 Maude parlayed her love of stage lighting into a job with General Electric Laboratories. She experimented with color lamps for movies. She invented a high-powered incandescent lamp that eventually made color movies possible. An electrical inventor at the lab filed a patent on the product, giv-ing her no credit at all for her contribution. She was advised to sue but refused to pursue litigation and later noted in her diary that she thought herself an "idiot" for the decision.

In 1915 Maude was forced to deal with a series of devastating tragedies. Her mother, grandmother, and manager all died within a short time of one another. The loss of Charles Frohman was particularly hard on the actress. He had been aboard the *Lusitania,* a passenger ship sunk by a German U-boat. Her grief over his death was a major factor in her decision to retire temporarily from acting. She was inde-pendently wealthy at this point in her career and could afford to do so. Before retir-ing altogether she was persuaded to return to the stage only two more times: Thirteen years after Charles's death she portrayed the character Portia in *The Merchant of Venice* in Ohio; her final stage performance was in 1934 at a theater in Maine, where she played Maria in *Twelfth Night.*

In 1937 Maude was invited to join the staff of Stephens, a junior college for girls in Columbia, Missouri, where she was the head of the drama department for six years. She retired from teaching in 1950 and moved to upstate New York, spending her days visiting with friends and writing. Three years later she was hospitalized with complications from pleurisy. Many cards and letters from well-wishers poured in. Though she had been out of the public eye for twenty years by this time, her fans had not forgotten her.

Maude Adams passed away on July 17, 1953, at her home in Tannersville, New York, at the age of eighty-one. She was buried in the private cemetery at Cenacle Convent in Ronkonkoma, Long Island. During her heyday she was the most popular actress in America.

Mary Anderson

SELF-MADE STAR

The angry hawk clenched its talons on the heavy leather gauntlet, stabbing the delicate wrist beneath. Wings bated, the half-wild bird glared fiercely into the large gray eyes of his captor. Mary Anderson stared back with steely determination. This unruly bird would be tamed, she resolved, and would become a living prop for her performance of the Countess in Sheridan Knowles's comedy, *Love.* A stuffed bird would not provide the realism she intended, and what Mary Anderson intended usually came to be.

"There is a fine hawking scene in one of the acts," Mary wrote in her memoirs, "which would have been spoiled by a stuffed falcon, however beautifully hooded and gyved he might have been; for to speak such words as: 'How nature fashion'd him for his bold trade, / Gave him his stars of eyes to range abroad, / His wings of glorious spread to mow the air, / And breast of might to use them' to an inanimate bird, would have been absurd," she declared. Always absolutely serious about her profession, Mary procured a half-wild bird and set to work on bending its spirit to her will.

The training, she explained, started with taking the hawk from a cage and feeding it raw meat "hoping thus to gain his affections." She wore heavy gloves and

MARY ANDERSON   1859–1940

goggles to protect her eyes. The hawk was not easily convinced of her motives and "painful scratches and tears were the only result."

She was advised to keep the bird from sleeping until its spirit broke, but she refused to take that course. Persevering with the original plan, Mary continued to feed and handle the hawk until it eventually learned to sit on her shoulder while she recited her lines, then fly to her wrist as she continued; then, at the signal from her hand, the bird would flap away as she concluded with a line about a glorious, dauntless bird.

The dauntless hawk and Mary Anderson were birds of a feather.

Born July 28, 1859, at a hotel in Sacramento, California, Mary's earliest years were unsettled. Her mother, Antonia Leugers, had eloped with Charles Henry Anderson, a young Englishman intent on finding his fortune in America. It was a love match not approved by Antonia's parents. The young couple arrived in Sacramento in time for Mary's birth but too late to scoop up a fortune from the nearest stream. The easy pickings of the 1849 Gold Rush were gone.

Disappointed, the family returned east to Louisville, Kentucky, where Mary's uncle was the priest in a small settlement near the city. Her father joined the Confederate Army and died in battle when she was three. A few years later her mother married Dr. Hamilton Griffin. Despite the strong guidance Griffin provided for his stepchildren, Mary, at least, went her headstrong way almost from the first.

"It was my desire to be always good and obedient, but, like 'Cousin Phoenix's legs,' my excellent intentions generally carried me in the opposite direction. On seeing a minstrel show for the first time I was fired with a desire to reproduce it. After a week of plotting with [my brother] Joe I invited Dr. Griffin and my mother to the performance of the nature of which they were utterly ignorant."

The performance took place in the family's front parlor, which was divided by double doors. The audience sat in back, and when the folding doors were thrown open, Mary's stunned parents took in the scene.

"My baby sister and I were discovered as 'end men.' She was but eight months old and tied to a chair. Our two small brothers sat between us, and we were all as black as burnt cork rubbed in by my managerial hands could make us." To top off the visual shock, Mary gaily began the opening chorus of the show: "Goodbye John! Don't stay long! Come back soon to your own chickabiddy."

That creative spirit and the will to back it up challenged the nuns at the Ursuline Convent Mary attended. They could not interest her in geography and arithmetic. "She was one of those children whose wild artist nature chafes under the restraints of home and school life," wrote J. M. Farrar of her early years. "Indeed, her wildness acquired for her the name of 'Little Mustang.'" The beautiful, headstrong little girl became a beautiful, headstrong woman who trained herself to become an actress who eventually became known in the western states as "Our Mary."

Mary was twelve years old and already memorizing Shakespeare when she saw the famous Shakespearean actor Edwin Booth in *Hamlet*. At that point The Bard became her self-selected schoolmaster, and becoming an actress became her one burning goal. At thirteen she dropped out of school and began studying elocution with a nearby teacher, but, above all, she memorized lines and practiced roles on her own.

Mary was about fifteen when she got hold of copies of old playbooks, which she used to teach herself. A local theater character, Uncle Henry Davis, an aged prompter from the days when performances included an offstage voice, or prompter, reading lines the actors repeated, provided her with an invaluable aid. Davis took apart the playbooks, added blank pages, and then diagrammed stage positions and described on them the "stage business" necessary to a performance. As she paced about, thinking, memorizing, trying to understand the motivations of Shakespeare's heroines, Mary unconsciously worried the yellow-backed books with her teeth.

Two years later, almost completely self-taught, Mary made her debut at a Louisville theater. On Saturday, November 27, 1875, after only a single rehearsal, she played Juliet before a packed house. The next morning the *Louisville Courier* praised her performance as a great actress but did not overlook her faults:

In the latter scenes she interpreted the very spirit and soul of tragedy, and thrilled the whole house into silence by the depth of her passion and her power. . . . We owe it to her, for it is the greatest kindness, and yet we do not speak harshly and are glad to admit that most of her faults—such for instance as frequently casting up the eyes—are not only slight in themselves, but enhanced if not caused by the timidity natural on such an occasion.

In February Mary again took the stage in Louisville, then opened in St. Louis and was invited to New Orleans, where, at the opening-night performance of *Evadne,* only 48 dollars was made in ticket sales. Nevertheless, young men in the audience from the military college nearby were so impressed by her beauty and passion that between acts they went out and bought up all the bouquets they could find—and the last act was played knee-deep in flowers. By the time she left New Orleans, the seventeen-year-old beauty was a star, and two Confederate generals and an admiring crowd saw her off at the train station.

Some criticism of her presentation appeared in newspapers and theater journals, but Mary was a sensation with the general public. It was early in 1876 when she, not yet eighteen, decided to tour the West. Accompanied by her mother and stepfather, Dr. Griffin, who was now managing her career, Mary declared her intention to bypass San Francisco for her first performance. Instead, she insisted on stopping first in the town of her birth, Sacramento. The people in the new state capital turned out to welcome her "home," but by the time she opened in San Francisco, she had acquired a few critics, some of whom considered her an empty-headed debutante like those in the city who wanted to become actresses. "We have some dozen or two in this little city alone," wrote an editor in the *San Francisco Call,* "and the dramatic fever is becoming as universal and epidemic as the epizooty among horses a season or two ago."

The work of self-taught actress Mary Anderson was often criticized in reviews, but western audiences were enamored with her performances.

Mary was hardly prepared for the reception she received from the press or the other actors in the troupe:

> My appearance in San Francisco at Mr. John McCullough's theatre soon followed, and was the most unhappy of my professional life. With but few exceptions, the members of the numerous company ridiculed my work. My poor wardrobe was a subject of special sport to the gorgeously dressed women; and unkind remarks about "the interloper" were heard on every side. The Press cut me up, or rather tried to cut me down, advising me to leave the stage. Continual taunts from actors and journalists nearly broke my spirit.

Mary was concerned for McCullough's ticket sales as well as the assault on her pride as an actress. On the last few nights she played Meg Merrilees in *Guy Mannering*, her ghostly makeup was so successful her own mother didn't recognize her. That role and one other dramatic part gained "genuine enthusiasm," the newspapers reported by the end of her San Francisco engagement.

Like the hawk she'd trained, her spirit had received a shock, but her will remained unbroken. In the midst of the terrible reviews in the press, her hero, Edwin Booth, appeared. "He laughed at my idea of quitting the stage on account of the unkindness of my fellow actors," she recalled. "I also am a fellow actor," said he; "I have sat through two of your performances from beginning to end—the first time I have done such a thing in years—and I have not only been interested, but impressed and delighted."

The remainder of the tour, which included an introduction to President Ulysses Grant, was highly successful. At her New York debut on November 12, 1877, she was considered to have "much dramatic potentiality." Her beauty was part of the attraction: "Tall, willowy and young," the *Herald* described, with a "fresh, fair face" and a small, finely chiseled mouth, large, almond-shaped eyes, and hair of light brown. She was beautiful, acknowledged the critics, but many found her lacking in feeling. One defender, however, spoke up on her behalf. Charles Wingate, author and historian, countered the prevailing opinion of Mary Anderson as cold or reserved:

> From the time of her first appearance on November 27, 1875, at McCauley's Theatre in Louisville, Ky., when the California-born girl was in her seventeenth year, her Juliet, her Rosalind, her Parthenia, her Galatea, her Pauline, her Julia, had shown what popular favor a magnificent figure, a superb voice, and a natural tragic power could gain, even if command of pathos and naturalness in comedy acting were less marked; but at the same time, the world constantly repeated the two words "cold" and "stately." Perdita, however, her last character on the stage, was a revelation.

Wingate described how Mary played two parts, one serious and rather austere, the other a light-footed "gazelle" who sang and danced with the abandon of a gypsy, something she had never successfully accomplished in the past.

By 1883 she was headed for Shakespeare's home ground in England, and she made it a point to put on performances in Stratford-on-Avon. She drew huge crowds and achieved unprecedented popular acclaim. Still, many of the British critics were not pleased by the American import.

She appeared as Galatea, a part that begins with the actress draped in white, gracefully posed, impersonating a beautiful marble statue that is brought to life by the love of the sculptor, Pygmalion. The critics said the part was easy because she played many of her parts with all the emotion of a statue. "Even in her ingenious scenes of comedy," reported the *Morning Post,* "there is no more dramatic vivacity than might be looked for in a block of stone."

Other newspapers realized how popular she had become. Despite the critics, Mary caught and held her audiences. "So strong was the appeal of her acting that on one occasion, where, as Galatea, she turned toward the auditorium with arms outstretched crying 'The Gods will help me,' the whole gallery rose and roared back 'We will! We will!'"

In 1886 she returned in triumph to America. Marcus R. Mayer, an advance agent drumming up publicity for her tour, told a reporter for the *San Francisco Call* that Mary was earning unprecedented sums. "Miss Anderson's gains have been simply immense," reported Mayer to the newspaperman. "She drew $249,000 during her seven months in London." Her receipts were larger, he said, than those of the famous Henry Irving and Ellen Terry, though she played in Mr. Irving's own theater. In New York she reportedly made $65,000, and three weeks in Boston netted $42,000. The entire tour in the East totaled $237,000, a huge sum of money in 1886.

The *Sacramento Union* published her itinerary: Denver, Salt Lake City, Sacramento, and then San Francisco. The second time around, San Francisco loved her. On April 4 the *San Francisco Call* detailed her training and its success: "The late Noble Butler grounded her in the use of the English language, and directed her literary work, besides developing her voice, the richness of which is one of her great charms. Mr. Wastell, the dancing master, taught her to dance and instructed her in posturing."

Mary described what she did to succeed at her chosen profession. She studied her characters and every word they uttered on stage and looked at the interaction between characters to pin down the psychology of her part. Physically, she worked hard at every move she performed. "Always on the alert for improvement," she said, she decided to try the Delsarte system of movement. " I determined to study it. As far as mechanical exercises were concerned, it seemed perfect to me, for it overlooks no muscle or tendon of the face or body, and gives strength, suppleness and control over them all. The rest of the system I afterwards found it best to discard."

One of the weak points of the system's theory, Mary decided, was the belief that outward expression and movement awaken and control emotions, which she concluded was exactly the opposite to what actually happened. "The development of these various types, with their natural personality, mannerisms, etc., is a most engrossing study. How would a man or woman weep under given circumstances? Would he or she weep at all? And so in joy as well as sorrow, under the influence of every emotion, they have their individual way of doing everything. The art is to make the character harmonious from beginning to end; and the greatest actor is he who loses his own personality in that of his *role*."

Since her days with the hawk, she had insisted on what was natural rather than melodramatic. Achieving that goal required deep analysis of reality and of the psychology of expression and emotion, with the aim of always portraying as true a character as possible.

Back in London in 1887, she presented a unique version of *The Winter's Tale*. It ran for 164 performances, and she played two parts, Hermione and Perdita, in each performance, something no other actress had attempted. In 1888 she brought the production back to America, but it ended abruptly in 1889. Some say Mary suffered a nervous breakdown. She herself put it differently;

> At Washington [it was Inauguration Week, and Mr. Harrison had just been proclaimed President] I went through the first two nights. On Ash Wednesday the doctor thought me too tired to make the effort, and I did not appear. On Thursday, against his wishes and those of that kindest of impresarios, Henry E. Abbey, I insisted on acting. The first scenes of *The Winter's Tale* went very smoothly. The theatre was crowded. Perdita [one of the parts she played] danced apparently as gaily as ever, but after the exertion, fell fainting from exhaustion, and was carried off the stage.

Mary explained that overwork caused the onstage blackout.

In *Shakespeare's Heroines of the Stage*, written in 1895, Charles Wingate wondered what might have happened had Mary not collapsed:

Curious it is to recall that one feature in this last stage character of Mary Anderson displayed for the first time an utter abandonment of the charge which, from the very first of her career, had been held up against her acting. All critics had admitted her natural beauty, all had commended her intelligence, and many had praised her for earnestness and strength. But all declared that she was cold and passionless.

Wingate found that Mary's final character had broken the mold:

> The quick-footed gazelle could scarcely have been more light of foot, more animated, or more fascinating in action. The wild gypsy-like dance showed a living picture of free, easy, voluptuous movement, so devoid of artificiality or restraint as to be as captivating as it was real for such an ideal country-bred character. Who could have believed the stately Mary Anderson capable of such graceful romping?

At twenty-four years old, Mary retired from the stage. In her memoirs she comments on the decision:

> After so much kindness from the public it seems ungrateful to confess that the practice of my art (not the study of it) had grown as time went on more and more distasteful to me.

Mary realized that being an actress was more than just immersing herself in her art—she recognized how the public came to feel an ownership interest in the life of an actor.

Speaking the words of Shakespeare, the poet who had awakened her to the dream of acting, had become a dull routine. She had been enamored with the characters wrought by Shakespeare's pen, and as a girl had never contemplated what success in portraying those characters might cost:

To be conscious that one's person was a target for any who paid to make it one; to live for months at a time in a groove, with uncongenial surroundings, and in an atmosphere seldom penetrated by the sun and air; and to be continually repeating the same passions and thoughts and the same words—that was the most part of my daily life, and became so like slavery.

With characteristic determination Mary Anderson retired at the peak of her popularity, just as she seemed to have overcome the one criticism that had dogged her career from the beginning. She had determined her course at the age of twelve, had worked to step onstage in a lead role and did it at barely seventeen; she'd traveled across the United States on tour several times, made a tremendous amount of money before she was twenty, had convinced the British Isles that an American could play Shakespeare, and had broken tradition by being the first actress to play two parts in *The Winter's Tale*.

In effect, Mary Anderson had no life but her life on the stage. She may have feared the same fate as the young hawk she'd once trained. "As an actor," she said of the hawk, "his career was highly successful. But constant travel and change of climate proved too much for him. In spite of the greatest care, he at last succumbed, and our noble bird was buried in the alley back of McVickers' Theatre, Chicago."

In June 1890 she married Antonio Fernando de Navarro, a wealthy American of Basque heritage who was said to have a claim on the throne of Spain. Mary met Tony when he arrived backstage after a performance. She'd refused his first requests to call on her but finally gave in and was impressed by the young man who looked and acted like a Spanish aristocrat. In her memoirs she recalls Tony telling her he vowed at that first meeting to marry her or become a priest.

The couple moved to Worcestershire, England. It was, according to her memoirs, a happy marriage that set her free from what she called bondage to the theater. She reveled in living naturally under the sun and the stars, rather than working to appear natural in a part written for a scene in a play performed under an artificial moon and fake stars suspended above the stage.

Mary and Tony were part of a wealthy, literate set that included famous writers, musicians, and playwrights. Their home was a mecca for artists, and Mary enjoyed riding and outdoor entertainments as well as domestic pursuits. Her first son died in infancy, but two other children prospered. Mary was continually asked to return to the stage, but her appearances were generally limited to charity work. During World War I she appeared on behalf of war charities and made visits to injured soldiers and to women working in factories to support the war effort.

Tony died in 1932, and Mary lived another eight years, the last several of which she was seriously ill. Mary died in 1940 at the age of eighty at her home in England.

Sarah Bernhardt

THE DIVINE SARAH

*With what the inhabitants of former worlds compared the sun,
I know not; and with whom the present generation may compare Bernhardt, I know as little.*

—*The Wave*, May 2, 1891

The pliant figure leaned over the ship's rail, expressive eyes intent on the blue-green waters of the harbor. A mass of wavy, light brown hair with tints of gold lifted and curled with every breeze, its arrangement a matter of complete indifference to the angler. Suddenly the slender form froze, breath held, and then, with a quick yank and a breaking smile, lifted the rod and hauled a wriggling fish aboard the *Cabrillo*. Exclaiming in French, dark eyes sparkling with pleasure, Sarah Bernhardt ordered her catch, small as it was, to be prepared for dinner.

It was May 19, 1906, and the farewell production of *Camille* was scheduled for a few hours later at the ocean auditorium built on the water at Venice, California. Sarah stayed, and fished, at the hotel built like a ship, and performed in the adjacent theater on the wharf at the seaside resort, Venice of America. Having caught a fish, Sarah wended her way to her quarters. Piled high in her dressing room were the results of a recent shopping trip to the Oriental bazaar nearby: silk and crepe matinee coats of pink and pale blue and mauve, all embroidered in butterflies and bamboo designs.

The tiny window in the dressing room provided a sparkling view of the

29

SARAH BERNHARDT 1844–1923

ocean, and the streaming sunshine picked out details of the furnishings: a repoussé silver powder box, containers of pigment, eyebrow pencils, silver rouge pots, and scattered jewelry twinkling in the light. The tragedienne who attracted huge audiences wherever she went swooped up a small tan and white fox terrier, wriggling with joy at her return, and snuggled it close for a moment as she related the happy details of her fishing venture to a visiting reporter. Then, she put down the small dog and closed her mind to the fun waiting outside the porthole.

Within moments Sarah became Marguerite Gautier, filled with the sadness and torment of the beautiful French courtesan in *Camille*, the play by Alexandre Dumas the younger that became her signature role, performed all over the world more than 3,000 times. Sarah's ability to sink fully into the character of the play made the tragic death scene so convincing that it became a trademark for "the Divine Sarah."

No one played tragedy with such believable intensity as Sarah Bernhardt, and no one brought as much passion and enthusiasm to the pursuit of pleasure. From fishing on the southern California coast to bear hunting in the woods outside Seattle, on every western tour the French actress indulged in some kind of adventure. Sarah Bernhardt threw herself into life with the same characteristic energy she put into her stage appearances. Yet she often slept in a coffin, preparing for that final sleep.

She was born in Paris, France, on October 23, 1844, the illegitimate daughter of milliner-cum-mistress Judith Van Hard and, probably, law student Edouard Bernard. Named Henriette-Rosine Bernard, she was a thin, sickly child, alternately deeply depressed or shouting with joy. Her dramatic nature revealed itself early. At the age of eight, seeing her aunt's carriage stopped in the street near the house where her mother had left her for months, and being forbidden to leave by her caretakers, she forced open a second-floor window and jumped out in front of the carriage. Although the fall resulted in a dislocated shoulder and shattered kneecap, her aunt was compelled to pay attention to the child's hysterical pleadings to be taken away.

Sarah could neither read nor write, and her behavior veered between opposite extremes of emotion, depending on her moods. The spectacular descent from the window achieved its goal: Her mother and her aunt decided something had to be done about her education. Her mother sent her to school, and later, with the help of the Duc de Morny, she was trained in dramatic arts and began her career at the Comédie Française.

Always frail, she nearly died from lung problems, and as a teenager, sure that she would not live long, Sarah nagged her mother into buying her a coffin so that she could get used to lying in it; photographs show her in quiet repose within the silk-lined box. Yet her passionate energy was revealed in the many altercations with other actresses and producers that made her first years in theater so difficult.

By 1864 the aspiring actress had met with some success. Severely afflicted with stage fright, which affected her all her life, some of her performances were uneven at best. Reviews were not terrible, but for a young woman who expected perfection, even modest phrases like "she carries herself well and pronounces her words with perfect clarity" seemed the epitome of insult.

After performing a bad part in a poor play, Sarah went to Brussels, where she met Prince Henri de Ligne. The affair resulted in pregnancy, followed by the birth of a son, Maurice. Some fifteen years later she still carried Maurice's first little shoes in her purse—they were once discovered by a customs inspector in the bottom of her handbag.

She didn't speak English, but that had not deterred British audiences from growing hysterical over her command of a tragic role. Her flamboyant lifestyle added to the reputation that carried her to triumph across the Channel. Reports of her menagerie, which included a lion, pictures of the opulent interior of her home, her jewels, her lovers, and the coffin in which she still sometimes slept, all fanned the imagination of the staid British public.

Her fame was immense in Europe by the time she first toured the United States in 1880. After early appearances in eastern states, where her adventures made headlines and huge crowds waited for a glimpse of the famous face and form, she

"The Divine Sarah" had a well-known adventurous side. She learned to fence for a role, went on a bear hunt while visiting Seattle, fished the Pacific Coast, and performed in tents and barns when finer sites were not available.

started west, playing in major cities like Salt Lake, Denver, and, finally, San Francisco. San Francisco's *Morning Call* of May 17, 1887, described the well-dressed throng that turned out for her first performance:

> When 8 o'clock arrived and the house was filled it was, in the words of the old-time usher "Gus," the best house the Baldwin has seen. Bob Eberle ran his arithmetical eye over the assemblage and put it down at over $4500. The ladies costumes were of the most elaborate order, even to the family circle, usually staid, but for this occasion brilliant in the sheen of silks and the glitter of diamonds.

The reviewer found not one wrong note in Bernhardt's appearance at the Baldwin Theater. In the May 30th edition of the paper, an accounting is provided that shows total receipts from her performances at nearly $41,400. But reporters found her exploits off the stage as compelling to write about as the tragedies she enacted.

Within a few years Sarah's extremely thin figure had been caricatured in Europe and America. Drawings of the actress in newspapers show a wraith figure crowned by a large head and masses of wild hair. The *Call* of April 1891 provided a full description of the famous actress and her lifestyle:

> In the Salon of 1876 Bernhardt's portrait was twice exhibited. One of the pictures shows her sitting in a white gown, slightly reclining on a sofa, and at her feet lies an immense dog. When Alexandre Dumas saw this portrait he remarked: "Un chien qui garde un os"; in English: "A dog watching a bone."

Despite the death's-head images that marked her fame, Sarah lived every moment with total intensity. The same reviewer in the *Call* described her frail constitution:

which does not, at the same time, prevent her from drawing largely on all the sources of enjoyment in life. She rides spirited horses and drives a fiery Russian span.

Finally, says the admiring reporter, she is "passionately fond" of fencing, which she learned in order to play a role that required she masquerade as a boy. That role may have been one of the most difficult she ever performed. In fact, without Sarah in the lead, Alfred de Musset's drama *Lorenzaccio* might not have been produced because it was considered too difficult to stage. It is based on a story from the dreaded Medici reign in Florence, Italy. In the play Sarah's role was that of the young Lorenzo, intent on ridding the city of the tyrant Alexander. As a correspondent in *The Argonaut* of 1897 wrote:

> She is the incarnation of the voluptuous, cynical, tigerish Foul Lorenzo. Every expression of face is a study. She has learned to walk, move, speak like a man. Not once does she betray her sex. In the fencing scene with Scoronconcocto, when the fury of hate and vengeance is upon the youth and he presses the bravo, half forgetful that it is not his abhorred enemy he holds at the point of his sword, Sarah is superb. It appears that at every rehearsal she donned male attire, that she might grow thoroughly accustomed to it, and the result is that she is as much at home in doublet and hose as if she had never worn a skirt in her life.

On the first night of the play, *The Argonaut* correspondent reported that the audience "reached delirium point:"

> I shall not soon forget the appearance of the house, the sound of the applause still rings in my ears, and I shall long be haunted by the vision of the panther-like form, mastered by the demon of murder, as it sprang on its sleeping victim.

At this time Sarah was fifty-two years old, yet no one considered her too old to take the lead in any play, even one so demanding as *Lorenzaccio*. Nor had her energy diminished; while she rehearsed the fencing scenes during the day, she performed every night in the original French version of *Camille*, even acting as stage manager between times.

The ability to convince her audiences that she was the person she represented in the role she played was made abundantly clear when she played Joan of Arc in her sixties. At one point in the play Joan is asked her age by a judge. "Nineteen," Sarah would say, turning slightly toward the audience, which, knowing the truth, sometimes stood up and cheered her ability to convince them of her youth.

A description of her appearance just after the turn of the century belies the skeleton caricature so long used to identify the actress. A reporter described the lines scribed by time and suffering in the famous countenance:

> Sarah Bernhardt is not precisely beautiful. She has deeply expressive blue eyes, white, even teeth, a fine nose whose nostrils nervously tremble in passion, and a purely chiseled chin. The best gift nature has bestowed upon her is her voice. This soft, deep organ is capable of unlimited modulation; its tones creep into the soul of the audience, and vaguely suggest a sultry evening breeze, or a warm, heavy fragrance of pinks. When she is on the stage her voice dominates the conversation as an organ does a church service.

Members of the clergy, on the other hand, were not so admiring of Sarah's performances. Bishops and ministers warned their flocks away from the dramas that she brought to life. The California editor of *The Wave* in 1891 defended her, however, explaining:

> It is not the fault of this woman that there is in the characters she represents—however baleful and obnoxious they

Sarah Bernhardt achieved worldwide acclaim for her intense dramatic stage performances.

may be—more dramatic value than in the village maiden. The genius of Bernhardt rarely makes the woman she represents loveable to those who see the representations; her La Tosca is a tigress, her Cleopatra a serpent, and her Camille a cat. As she portrays them we pity them for their sufferings, but abhor them for their deeds.

Sarah had a hard time understanding the objections to the characters in plays such as *Camille,* which she performed repeatedly in America. "This play, that the public rushed to see in crowds, shocked the overstrained Puritanism of the small American states," she wrote. "The critics of the large cities discussed this modern Magdalene. But those of the small towns began by throwing stones at her. This stilted reserve on the part of the public, prejudiced against Marguerite Gautier, we met from time to time in the small cities." For Sarah a town of 30,000 was "small."

"Quand même" was Sarah's motto. The phrase means roughly "in spite of everything," and it described her feisty nature perfectly. She adopted the motto at the age of nine after accepting a dare to jump a ditch, which resulted in a fall and a sprained wrist. She insisted she would do it again if dared. If nothing else in her long, adventurous life, she always dared.

While on her first tour of America, she went to the manufacturer and bought a Colt revolver. This was not an empty gesture designed for publicity. When an attempt was made to rob her train of the jewels and money it was said to contain, her "pretty little revolver" ornamented with cat's-eye stones did not have to be used, as a guard apprehended the thief. Sarah's revolver, however, was not just an unusual accessory. She was a good shot. While in Seattle, she went on a bear hunt and returned without a bear, but carrying a gray squirrel and several birds.

Traveling in a special "Palace Car," she crisscrossed America many times. In one season she made 156 appearances in fifty cities and towns. The luxurious railcar was embellished with walls of inlaid wood, lit by brass gas lamps, and furnished with splendid carpets, sofas, a piano, and potted palms. Ten people could be seated at the dining table, and two chefs prepared meals.

Her tour up the coast of California in 1906 avoided San Francisco, still cooling after the earthquake that had destroyed so much of the famed city just a few days earlier. Instead, she played for 7,000 people at the Greek Theater across the Bay at Berkeley. The interview published by *The Theatre Magazine* the following month delved deeply into Sarah's preparation for her roles. "I read the piece through, and yes, the interpretation of the character I am to play comes to me at once when first I read over the play," she replied in answer to a question. "I see it as it is to be done at once. If I cannot feel the part," and here, says the interviewer, she pressed her jeweled hands to her heart, "if I cannot feel the part I reject the play. I know instantly. If I do not catch the feeling I will not touch the piece."

Except in California her 1906 tour of the West was complicated by a syndicate of theater owners that refused to book her into their houses for economic reasons: Whichever theater signed Bernhardt got all the crowds while the other houses stood empty. Always aided by clever managers, Sarah instead played in whatever hall was available, including tents, all across the Southwest. Such was her fame by then that, it's said, a Texas cowboy demanded entrance at six-gun point to a sold-out house; inside he asked what this French "gal" did—sing or dance?

Farther north, in Butte, Montana, Sarah played in a huge, unheated roller-skating rink. Fewer than 1,200 people bought tickets. Canceling the appearance was discussed, but Sarah insisted the show go on, even though there would be no profits. The *Anaconda Standard* of May 6, 1906, noted that the Holland rink was freezing, that the actors appeared in furs, and that the people in the audience were wrapped up against the cold. As if that were not enough to discourage even the hardiest drama lover, "halfway down the hall not a sound from the stage could be heard," said the *Standard*. Still, at the end of the final act, "The freezing audience was as enthusiastic and warm as it could be, and the great actress was called before the stage repeatedly."

It was her only appearance that year in Montana. The *Standard* continued: "Mme. Bernhardt's farewell appearance in Butte was under extreme difficulties, but there are at least a thousand people who are glad they had the privilege and opportunity to see her again and once more sit under the spell of her genius."

A captive audience in 1913 sat rapt as she read for 2,000 inmates at San Quentin prison. Between engagements in San Francisco, Sarah performed her son's play, *Une Nuit de Noël sous la Terreur* (A Christmas Night under the Terror). It concludes with prisoners being released from the infamous French prison, the Bastille. Played in the prison yard crowded with men standing in striped uniforms, Sarah enthralled her audience. A letter from the prisoners thanked her for an hour's "perfect liberty" despite the high walls and the treacherous waters that kept the inmates confined.

Ever ready for adventure, during that same visit Sarah flew out over the Bay in a two-seater aircraft that promised the ultimate in freedom.

Two years later Sarah's own independence was threatened. She had suffered intermittently for years from a series of injuries to her right knee. The most disabling occurred in Rio de Janeiro in October 1905. During the last act of *La Tosca* she was required to fling herself from the parapet of a prison. Mattresses to cushion the fall on the other side had been misplaced, and Sarah landed hard on the already weak right knee. She declined treatment in South America and departed for New York. She couldn't walk for weeks but resumed her American tour in November, playing sixty-two cities.

The damaged knee never healed properly. Later, walking became so painful that sets were rearranged to provide support as she crossed the stage. By 1915 gangrene had set in, and Sarah, then seventy-one and suffering from chronic uremia, insisted the leg be amputated. Doctors declined until she threatened to shoot herself in the knee if they didn't do as she asked. Finally, one surgeon agreed. She reportedly went under the knife singing the French national anthem, "La Marseillaise."

Disliking the prosthetic device that would allow her to be somewhat mobile,

At the height of her fame, Sarah Bernhardt traveled America in a luxurious private railroad car complete with carpets, sofas, a piano, and potted palms.

the woman known for her sinuous grace and feline movements continued playing scenes from the roles she'd made famous, but she stayed in one place to do it. Sitting, reclining on a couch, or standing beside a prop, she used her voice, her hands, and all the intensity she could command to carry her audience away. Refusing the indignity of a wheelchair, she had a special litter chair built, complete with gilded carvings, in which she was carried about like royalty.

Despite her missing limb she visited troops near Verdun, not far from the front lines, where soldiers were engaged in bloody battles of World War I. Performing in whatever accommodation she could find—from mess tents to barns—she recited patriotic pieces for the French troopers, who rose in waves to cheer their one-legged goddess. She returned to America in 1916 to recoup her fortunes, but a year later spent four months sidelined by kidney problems that required surgery.

Despite changes in theatrical tastes, Sarah Bernhardt never retired. Vaudeville was not too low for "the Divine Sarah." Instead of performing complete plays, she reprised scenes she'd made famous. The shorter format fit the customary vaudeville bill, which included everything from trained-animal acts to black-face minstrels. Unable to use the gestures and sinuous postures that were so much a part of her fame, she relied on her masterful voice, moments of silence, or a single lift of the hand to convey her meaning, and audiences responded deliriously.

Sarah was also seen on the silent screen. Her first cinema appearance was at the Paris Exposition in 1900. By then she was sixty-six years old, yet her interest in the new medium continued until her death in 1923. She made eight films. Her biggest hit was *Queen Elizabeth,* and she was shooting a film on location when she collapsed. She died on March 26, in the arms of her son, Maurice, and that evening theaters in Paris paid silent homage for two minutes. She was buried in the rosewood coffin her mother had purchased at her insistence when she was but fifteen years old, sure that her life would be tragically short.

Mrs. Leslie Carter

PASSIONATE PLAYER

My life has run in strange places. My years have been full of color. I have known the heights of success, but likewise I have known the depths of despair.

—Mrs. Leslie Carter, *Liberty Magazine*, 1927

Catherine Louise Dudley Carter sat at her desk and clutched a pen in her hand. Nothing was left of her life but the raw will to do the only quasi-respectable thing open to a woman in her circumstances. She had lost the wealthy position and standing in society that she had taken for granted for so long. She'd been kicked out of her palatial home. She had failed in her divorce case and in obtaining the money to maintain her lifestyle; her nine-year-old son had been ripped from her arms, and her once good name had been scandalously linked to actor Kyrle Bellew and New York Senator James F. Pierce.

The scandal didn't bother her too much—small-minded persons, including her husband, just did not understand. "There is great romance, there is great love, there is great passion—all things difficult to guide—and some men and women reserve the right to have these things, regardless of that sharp dividing line which makes it legal," she later wrote, dramatically justifying her choices.

Unfortunately, she'd fallen to the wrong side of that sharp legal and moral dividing line and now knew the cost. Her husband, wealthy industrialist Leslie

MRS. LESLIE CARTER   1862–1937

Carter, had won everything in what the *New York Times*, in June of 1889, called the "most indecent and revolting divorce trial ever heard in the Chicago courts." Louise Carter considered herself virtually penniless, her reputation shredded to ribbons by the press, while her husband gloated over winning his countersuit, charging her with adultery.

She shuddered at the memory of the witnesses against her, a veritable parade of chambermaids, housekeepers, hotel guests, and other traitors her husband had somehow coerced into telling the most awful tales about her. He had taken everything from her. She decided to take the one thing he'd given her that could most embarrass him: his name.

The plan she conceived to become an actress did not stop short of stardom. Her name—no, his name— would be blazoned in lights for all to see. She would, forevermore, be known as Mrs. Leslie Carter. That, she thought, would make her husband's impassive face show some expression. "Nothing ever happened to Leslie Carter; consequently, nothing ever happened to his face," she recalled. The day would come, she vowed, when the name she hated would be on marquee lights and his humiliation would be as great as hers was now.

Dreaming of revenge would not make it happen. Images of poverty and squalor rose in her mind. Somehow she must triumph over this ugly trick of fate that her husband and a jury had played. The theater offered the only way out, with the added attraction of mortifying her ex-husband. Shrugging away the fact that her first attempt at becoming an actress had been unsuccessful, she concocted a new plan to succeed.

Dipping her pen into a small bottle of ink, she wrote to a man who had promised to help. The plea Louise Carter sent to wealthy meat packer Nathaniel K. Fairbank resulted in an offer to assist her to become an actress, and his influence secured an appointment with New York theatrical manager E. G. Gilmore, who agreed to handle her career.

The theater community was not just astonished by the reports that the sinful society woman intended to take to the stage; it was dumbfounded. Louise Carter had nothing much to recommend her, except, possibly, the notoriety she'd gained in the press. With no particular beauty, an astonishing amount of wild red hair, strong features, an unsavory reputation, and complete ignorance of her chosen profession, it seemed hardly feasible that she could join the ranks of Sarah Bernhardt and Lillie Langtry, reigning stars of the theater in 1889.

Her family tree showed not a twig or branch from the theatrical profession. She was born June 10, 1862, in Lexington, Kentucky. Her father was a dry-goods merchant, and Catherine Louise was the younger of two children. Following her father's death when she was eight years old, her mother took the children to Dayton, Ohio, where their grandfather lived. There, the lively young redhead had been a student at the Cooper Seminary, where she was very popular with her classmates and the wealthy young gentlemen who came to call.

At the age of eighteen, she married the millionaire industrialist Leslie Carter, who was fourteen years her senior. The marriage was arranged by her mother and a family friend, and Catherine Louise agreed to it because it was expected. "There are certain events that arrived in due course in life," she said, and marriage was inevitable for a young woman of good family.

She returned with her husband to his hometown of Chicago, where she played her role as the wife of an important man in society. The newlyweds, however, were not alone in the Chicago mansion; Leslie Carter's brother, his aunt, and his sister also lived there. "Here was this somber house filled to the brim with prejudices, conventionalities and prohibitions," she described later. The aunt and sister were not "bachelor girls or old maids, but spinsters." The self-described "hoyden" was "continually affronting and offending without knowing how or why."

One good thing about the divorce was that she was finally free of the family ties, which had become chains. Catherine Louise Carter was pleased to think that becoming an actress would be one last rude gesture toward her husband's family. With the newspapers screaming her name and the future uncertain at best, however, everyone, including her wealthy sponsor, considered her ideas about a career extremely improbable, so she set her sights on the one man who could make it happen.

The legendary David Belasco had earned his actor's laurels in San Francisco theater productions in the 1870s and in Virginia City, Nevada, where he first began writing plays that were moderately successful. Unfortunately, his initial meeting with the society woman who thought she might like to be an actress had not gone well. He wrote, "When she first came to my attention she had no training for the stage, though as a young girl she had appeared in a number of school plays. She was bent upon becoming an actress, but she expected to start at the top. She did not have the slightest notion of what is demanded for a successful career on the stage."

Belasco had asked her whether she had in mind training for comedy or for tragedy. Her reply only confirmed his doubts about her commitment to the acting profession. "I am a horsewoman and I should like to make my first entrance on horseback jumping a high fence," she arrogantly announced.

Belasco, with a reputation for withering the hopes of the pretentious, explained what it would take to prepare for a serious career in theater and was convinced at the close of their interview that he would never see Mrs. Carter behind the footlights. Thinking the matter ended, he left town. He seriously underestimated her will. Showing the determination that anchored her wildly passionate nature, she set off for Belasco's rural hideaway, where he was working on a play for the Lyceum Theatre Company. There, on bended knee, she begged for his help. "If being hurt by people can make me act, I can act," she cried, tears rolling down her cheeks.

Belasco later described the meeting in *The Theatre Through Its Stage Door*. Before him knelt a plain woman, he said, slender and graceful. Her hair was thick and red, her eyes green under dark eyebrows, her expression beseeching. "Nothing about her was beautiful or even pretty, but the radiance of her features, the eloquence of her soul, and the magnetism of her highly keyed, temperamental nature convinced me then and there that she would go far, if only her natural abilities were developed and controlled."

Belasco and Mrs. Carter were in some ways mirror images. He'd noted at their first meeting the intensity of her emotions, and as actor, producer, and playwright, Belasco often displayed his own remarkably intense nature. He told the story of visiting a San Francisco medical college, where he stood like a statue staring at the dissected heart of a woman who had committed suicide after resorting to prostitution. Sitting for several hours on a hard bench, gazing at the permanently still heart, he sank himself emotionally into the grief that had driven the woman to take her own life. Whenever he needed to call up deep, emotional energies, he said he would picture that small heart lying silent on an autopsy table.

Using his own tried-and-true methods of evoking intense feelings, Belasco almost forcibly created an actress from a society debutante. In November 1890, after the divorce case had concluded in blaring headlines, with the, by then, reluctant backing of theatrical "angel" N. K. Fairbank, Mrs. Leslie Carter made her debut in the aptly named play *The Ugly Duckling.* The play had little to commend it in the first place and had been doctored by a professional rewrite artist; that effort not hatching a swan, Belasco had added his own hand to the script.

Theater reporters agreed the play was deadly. The critics were not altogether harsh with the fledgling actress following the opening-night performance. The *New York Times,* which had charged the Chicago press with yellow journalism in editorials warning that women and children should not read the newspaper accounts of the divorce, noted the scandal but acknowledged that Mrs. Carter could, in time, become a "useful actress."

Not exactly the praise that Mrs. Leslie Carter expected, but better than a barrage of overripe vegetables. Behind the scenes, however, Catherine Louise was hanging on by a thread. The wealthy pork magnate backing her career had tightened the purse strings. Belasco had not been paid, nor had the dance and voice coaches, the scenery painters, and sundry others associated with staging a production. And of course there was the wardrobe she required. In a letter to Fairbank's lawyer, Charles L. Allen, she pleaded Belasco's case and then itemized her own needs: $3,000 for dresses, purchased, of course, in Europe and $140 for living expenses each month, plus the weekly charges for all her classes in singing, dancing, elocution, etc. At the end of the list, she nobly remarked that she had gone hungry more than once but didn't mind the lack of food. All her energy was concentrated in one goal: succeeding on stage.

Enough money was scraped up to present *The Ugly Duckling*, but Fairbank had cut off greater funding, and when the company took the production on the road and played to empty houses, they ended up begging their "theatrical angel" for enough money to play Chicago. He at first refused, then gave in after Belasco reportedly threatened to tell the story to the newspapers. Fairbank came up with the money, the show went on for two weeks, and Mrs. Carter netted some cash, whereas Fairbank received nothing on his investment.

Having been launched to tepid praise and after barely surviving the financially ruinous road trips at small theaters in the East, Belasco and Carter were far from the big time. It wasn't until several years later, when she appeared in *The Heart of Maryland*, a Civil War drama written for her by Belasco, that she gained credit as a dramatic or "emotional" actress.

The play demanded a lot from a performer playing the lead in the drama Belasco had concocted, but for Mrs. Leslie Carter, drama was a way of life. In the most thrilling moment of the play, she climbed a 40-foot bell tower and grasped the bell clapper to keep it from ringing and betraying the location of the hero, who made his escape while she swung to and fro above the scenery. That scene had the audience on its feet. The play was a smash.

But her notoriety sometimes eclipsed her performance. When the production was staged in California, *The Argonaut* recognized the actress's past even as it spoke well of her future. "The star is Mrs. Leslie Carter, who has impersonated the title role since the beginning. She began her stage career with little other capital than a divorce scandal, but she is now acknowledged to be an excellent emotional actress. How she became so we all know from Mr. Belasco's testimony in the trial he brought against Mr. Fairbank, the Chicago 'angel' who launched her in her career."

There was the bitter and the sweet in her new success. Finally, the vow she'd sworn to get even with her ex-husband was realized: "Electric lights over the theater lobbies will carry the name of Leslie Carter in five foot letters. I hate the name; consequently, I will bear it to the end. Newspapers shall spread it forth, the streets shall hum with it. Mrs. Leslie Carter! It shall be borne upon him by the printed word and the spoken word. He cannot escape. It shall hound him until his last day!"

Mr. Leslie Carter reportedly could not have cared less. "I'll never speak or listen to the mention of her name again," he announced. In later years, however, when she returned to play in Chicago, posters bearing the actress's name were kept from his sight, and he often left town during a run of her show.

At last she had her revenge. She'd lost the divorce, lost her child, lost everything but that indomitable will to get to the top. No matter what he said, she knew exactly how galling it would be to Leslie Carter to have his name a public commodity associated not with his wealth and prestige, but with his despised ex-wife's notorious lifestyle.

Perhaps her husband had misjudged her will to succeed. Without it she could not have survived Belasco's methods, as noted in the *Argonaut's* review of *The Heart of Maryland*. Belasco had described his training of Louise Dudley Carter in a court proceeding against Fairbank, the meat packer who had bankrolled her training as well as her first play. Although that trial took place in New York, it made headlines all over the country. Belasco, testifying in the case, said he had taken a society woman, a crude amateur, and taught her everything, from how to walk into a room to how to cry, how to read a letter, how to sit down, how to open a book, virtually every physical and emotional action, including how to breathe.

Indeed, his methods were reported with great relish by the newspapers as the trial continued. His description of training Mrs. Carter to play a scene from *Oliver Twist* had the jurors gaping, according to the press. "I dragged her around by her hair, just as Bill Sykes dragged Nancy. I would hit her head on the floor and haul her about until she had reached the proper pitch and could express just what she felt."

In Belasco's view he had more than earned the money he demanded from Fairbank. "I instructed her in thirty or forty roles. She was taught fencing, boxing, wrestling and dancing; she learned ballet and jig dancing, I taught her to be the embodiment of the poetry of motion—a great nerve trial."

At the end of the three-week court trial, Belasco was awarded only a small portion of the sum for which he sued Fairbank. The *New York Times* published a scathing editorial against the jurors and the verdict, which gave Belasco $16,000 instead of the $55,000 he had claimed as the trainer of a great "emotional actress."

The training may have actually been worth every penny that Belasco claimed. A few years later, while touring in the western states, the *San Francisco Chronicle* noted: "Mrs. Carter reaches a degree of febrile intensity which is tremendously effective."

After an extensive tour in 1906, Louise Carter decided to take some time off. Her red-haired son had left his father's straight-laced household as soon as he was old enough and joined his mother, despite being disinherited for deserting to the enemy camp. With her son and some friends, she traveled to the Atlantic coast and there took a step that would dramatically change her life. While she was vacationing in Portsmouth, Massachusetts, she suddenly married actor William Louis Payne. When the news reached David Belasco, he refused to believe it. "I would as soon think of the devil asking for holy water as Mrs. Carter taking a husband," Belasco was quoted as saying when the rumors about his star began circulating.

When the gossip proved true, in perfect accord with his own dramatic reputation, Belasco telephoned the new Mrs. William Payne and told her that would be the last time she would be privileged to hear his voice. As fiercely determined as Mrs. Carter had been, he immediately began grooming a new star.

Over the next few years, without Belasco writing and producing new plays especially for her and without him drawing out every last breath of emotion possible from the actress he'd created from a willful debutante, Mrs. Carter's career declined. She performed roles Belasco had created for her in plays such as *Zaza* and *DuBarry*, but the critics were left unsatisfied.

"*DuBarry*, in which Mrs. Leslie Carter is performing at the Grand Opera House in San Francisco, is not a pleasant play; but if nothing in its plot can please— in the highest sense of the word—Mrs. Carter certainly does succeed in attracting and fascinating her auditor, and this she does by her virile force as an actress. Lacking the charm which makes Maude Adams, for instance, loved by the public, she never- theless compels a species of admiration," wrote a reviewer in *Sunset Magazine*.

The critic could not quite pinpoint what it was about Mrs. Carter that didn't quite make the grade: "Great she is not—something is lacking to that high distinc- tion—but she so nearly attains greatness that the average witness of her acting is not quite certain whether or not she falls short of it. Only an uncomfortable conviction that something was lacking remains with him, and, even at the height of his admi- ration for her art, will not be dissipated."

Having started her own production company and taken her show on the road, the actress soon learned the realities of a budget. By 1908 Mrs. Carter was forced into bankruptcy, with debts amounting to nearly $200,000. An auction of her belongings attracted a throng of women who both admired and scorned her. The ugly divorce scandal had never completely faded away, and even her success was somehow held against her. In 1916 she announced her retirement and settled in England with her second husband, but she eventually made a comeback.

Her last really successful appearance on stage occurred in 1921. Ironically, she was often competing against herself. A movie had been made of *The Heart of Maryland*, the vehicle that had made her a star, but she had no part in it. Too often her audi- ences were small because the movie was playing during the run of her live shows.

Bowing to the inevitable lure of the movies, she was performing character roles in Hollywood by 1931. Her son Dudley died a few years later, leaving her once more a victim of emotional anguish. One other terrible sorrow plagued her last years. She and Belasco never healed the rift caused by her marriage to William Payne.

She had written her mentor repeatedly begging for reconciliation. He refused, and once, the story goes, finding himself face to face in the same elevator with the actress he'd molded, he stared stonily ahead and refused to acknowledge her presence.

Gone was the admiration that had impelled Belasco to undertake the training of a society sophisticate. Erased was the memory of the "pale, slender girl with a mass of red hair and green eyes gleaming under black brows, her gestures full of unconscious grace and her voice vibrated with a musical sweetness." Gone was the convoluted dependency that had brought them both such success.

David Belasco died in May 1931 without responding to the many letters sent to him by his protégé.

She wrote a final testimonial. "We fought together years and years obstacles that seemed insurmountable, but his belief in me and my absolute sublime faith in him always helped us smile and look ahead with courage. And it seems so awful that he should have to lose this last fight." And then she quoted lines Belasco had written:

> The soul is a very lonely thing —
> lonely comes it here—lonely goes it there—
> a cry at night among the trees—
> a glimmer in the mist that soon goes out—
> a little shriek of passing wind—and then
> it goes up on its journey—where?

Catherine Louise Carter died in November 1937 of a heart ailment aggravated by pneumonia. Her former leading man and second husband, William Payne, the man who had come between her and Belasco, was by her side.

In 1942 Miriam Hopkins and Claude Rains starred in the movie production of *The Woman with Red Hair,* the story of the tempestuous relationship of Mrs. Leslie Carter and David Belasco.

Caroline Chapman

SHAKESPEARE TO SLAPSTICK

We sincerely question if there ever was an actress more perfectly at home upon the stage than Miss Chapman.

—*Alta California*, San Francisco, May 24, 1853

The theater at Camp Seco, a gold camp in California, could hardly compare to the Greenwich Theater in New York, or the Jenny Lind in San Francisco, or theaters in New Orleans, Philadelphia, or other cities she'd played in, but Caroline Chapman had rarely seen a more enthusiastic audience. Twitching her skirts into place, she waited for her cue. Tonight they would conclude the program with a spoof of notorious entertainer Lola Montez, an act that always brought down the house.

Caroline and her brother, "Uncle Billy" Chapman, had left San Francisco in an uproar after starring in a hilarious play by Dr. Robinson. Newspaper editors had sharp words for *Who's Got the Countess?* and Caroline's part in it. How, they asked, could the "modest" Miss Caroline Chapman descend to such tasteless, even cruel burlesque of the lovely Lola?

That was easy, Caroline thought. She was a professional actress, and as she waited for her cue, she could balance that accomplishment against a lack of beauty that had also been politely noted in the press. Critics admired Lola's stunning face and form, but few of them considered her a serious actress. Lola's stage career in Europe had included a stint as the mistress of the King of Bavaria, who had made

CAROLINE CHAPMAN   1818–1876

her Countess of Landsfelt. Caroline, on the other hand, had started learning stage work as a child on her father's riverboat and had garnered praise from her first performance.

Beauty was not Caroline's stock in trade. Caroline was too plain to compete with the legendary Lola's charms. The most complimentary report on her appearance had come from theater historian Joseph Ireland, who described her as slender and plain-featured but with excellent teeth in a large, mobile mouth. Her face was radiant with expression communicated by a pair of gleaming dark eyes that could convey more meaning, either of mirth or sadness, said Ireland, than any contemporary female on the New York stage.

And, unlike the scandalous Lola, Caroline had never indulged in affairs with royalty or famous authors and had never smoked a cigar, kept a pet bear, or threatened to take a riding whip to a cynical newspaper editor. Caroline Chapman had what Lola lacked: talent. Nowhere did she find it more fun to exhibit than in Dr. Robinson's send-up of the glamorous Countess of Landsfelt, whose stage reputation depended more on her display of shapely legs than on a demonstration of acting ability.

Lola became famous for her Spider Dance—a frantic effort to shake blackened cork "spiders" from her skirts that required lifting and shaking of dress and petticoats—which shocked the polite world but attracted droves of admirers to the theater. Lola's well-attended appearances in San Francisco in 1853 inspired local theatrical entrepreneur Dr. G. C. Robinson to pen the hilarious farce, *Who's Got the Countess?* in which Caroline performed.

"Some weeks ago the Countess came to fill us with delight, / And drew admiring throngs to see her spider dance each night. . . ." As Dr. Robinson's familiar song rang out over the heads of miners crowded into the makeshift theater, Caroline swirled haughtily onstage. She might not be beautiful, but she could act rings around the likes of Lola Montez.

Reviews showering praise on Caroline and Uncle Billy and their repertoire filled newspapers across the state. The *Daily Alta California* in December 1853 reviewed Caroline's appearance at the American Theater:

> She has never had an equal. In either genteel or low comedy she far excels all others, and it matters not whether singing, dancing, or acting is required, she is equally proficient in all, and brings the highest cultivation and most graceful native qualities to the performances.

Born in 1818 into a dynasty of actors and producers that were famous at Haymarket and Covent Garden theaters in England, Caroline learned the acting craft in America after her father brought the family to New York. In 1831 Caroline's father, William Chapman, procured a large flatboat and turned it into a theater in which his family members were the players. Caroline started her career aboard Chapman's Floating Palace, the riverboat playhouse that may have been the first of its kind on the Mississippi. At about the age of eleven, Caroline stepped onstage to support the family's theatrical adventures at the American Opera House in New York.

The Chapman family was chock-full of actors, and the troupe plied the Mississippi for years before William Chapman died and many members of the family headed for the bustling streets of San Francisco. Caroline made her debut in New York as an adult in 1846. Her skills were favorably noted when she played in *A Husband at First Sight* at the age of twenty-eight at the Greenwich Theater.

She was thirty-two years old when she and her older brother, who became known as "Uncle Billy," arrived in San Francisco in 1850. According to some accounts Uncle Billy may have been Caroline's father rather than her brother. Whatever the truth about their kinship, the duo became popular performers as soon as they hit the boards in the City by the Bay.

San Francisco was the jumping-off point for the goldfields. The sprawling territory of California was scarcely two years old, carried to statehood on the strength of the Gold Rush, which was luring thousands of young men from all over the world to the foothills of the Sierra Nevada. Many of these argonauts were well educated and well traveled, and they knew their Shakespeare. Miners and the merchants who catered to them would line up outside a makeshift theater, dressed in their best, to buy an expensive ticket for a seat on a plank bench just to watch an itinerant troupe of actors perform *Hamlet* or *Romeo and Juliet*. If the show did not meet their expectations, the scruffy audiences were not above pitching ripe fruit at the players.

Caroline became an instant success with her first appearance in 1852 at Tom Maguire's imposing new Jenny Lind Theater, the third incarnation of the playhouse.

The first Jenny Lind Theater was built by impresario Tom Maguire on the floor above a gambling den called the Parker House Saloon in Portsmouth Square. In 1850 Maguire's first San Francisco theater had seemed a vast improvement over some others that were little more than rickety wooden structures, sometimes lacking a floor, and roofed with canvas. Some barnstormers traveling between mining camps entertained in tents, saloons, and barns, with makeshift scenery and shoddy costumes.

By contrast, at the first Jenny Lind, patrons were enclosed within deep-rose wall panels, seated in gilded boxes from which they looked out on a painted drop curtain that was hung to set the scene.

Unfortunately, all that splendor disappeared when, in May 1851, the Jenny Lind burned to the ground along with a large section of the city always prone to fire. Maguire immediately rebuilt and reopened on June 13; nine days later, however, only embers remained. Once again the indefatigable Maguire rebuilt, this time in a more permanent fashion.

Caroline Chapman's first appearance in San Francisco was at the third, and most opulent, Jenny Lind Theater. The *Herald* said it was the "largest and handsomest building in the city." Built of brick with a white sandstone exterior imported from Australia, the new Jenny Lind was three stories tall and contained 2,000 seats including a balcony, galleries, opulent boxes, orchestra stalls, and a dress circle. Caroline's initial performance in late spring of 1852 was well received, and during the remainder of the season she showed her versatility in drama as well as farcical afterpieces.

Leaving the plush Jenny Lind behind in 1853, she and Uncle Billy made a tour of the mines. They were a smash hit from Nevada City to Sonora and points between. Although the weather was dismal at best, with torrential rains and heavy snowfall, the lighthearted actors brought sunshine and left with gold-lined pockets.

The Mother Lode region had something that made it an ideal venue for a popular actress: red-shirted miners hungry for entertainment, their "pokes" filled with spending money measured by the ounce. Gold dust in small leather bags landed with pleasing regularity at the feet of the actress following a performance.

The primitive stages in gold camps did not daunt this professional who had learned her craft in the small wooden structure nailed to her father's first flatboat theater. The editors of *A History of Tuolumne County* described the playhouse where the Chapman troupe played in 1853 as consisting of wood planks nailed together to make the walls, the whole covered by canvas, with, of course, a barroom through which patrons had to pass to reach the wood benches placed before the stage:

> In this primitive structure the Chapman Family held forth for many nights, playing the initial engagement. These actors seem to have had an exceedingly successful season in the mines, playing in all the camps which contained any facilities for such performances, or men enough to compose an audience. Every man went to hear them, and very possibly no actors, "star" or otherwise, ever met the expectations of their audiences more fully; and certainly no audiences ever rose to the demands of the performers with such unanimity—such excess of satisfaction and ebullition of feeling—as theirs. At Columbia the stage was covered with buckskin purses, each containing what the generous givers thought a proper testimonial.

According to the article, tossing pokes of gold at the feet of the company lacked the pleasing resonance the miners felt appropriate to the occasion. "Discovering, however, that there was not noise enough about it to fully emphasize their feelings, the boys took to throwing silver pieces, and there was, it was said, an immediate scarcity of these coins, which, by the way, had not long been in circulation."

The Phoenix Theater in Sonora advertised a grand opening on New Year's night with a full orchestra and a "powerful" company headed by Miss Caroline Chapman. It is said that more than a thousand miners acted as escort as the Chapmans traveled the 5 miles from Columbia to Sonora. Caroline delivered an opening address, then played with Uncle Billy in the three-act comedy *The Serious Family*, which was followed by dancing and singing. The program concluded with a favorite farce, *Rough Diamond*.

Following the triumphant and lucrative tour of the mines, in late 1853 Caroline returned to San Francisco, where she continued to please audiences. Playing opposite the young Edwin Booth (brother to John Wilkes Booth, who later assassinated Abraham Lincoln), Caroline displayed her talent well in a variety of roles. It was predicted that Edwin Booth would have an excellent career, based on his early years in San Francisco, but Caroline Chapman reached her zenith there.

In May 1853 the *Alta California* noted her many virtues:

> In everything where versatility and tact can be displayed—
> where sprightly vivacity and laughing wit appear, singing,
> dancing, and acting are all required, she probably has no
> equal on the American boards. There is a laughing good
> humor evinced on all proper occasions, which says, "I enjoy
> this, don't you?" in such a way that an audience cannot help
> but be pleased from mere sympathy. Everything of the light
> and airy kind she enters into with that ease and freedom
> which seems to say that she is living and not acting the char-
> acter in which she appears.

A benefit for the Union Grammar School in 1856 brought Caroline to the stage in one of the plays that demonstrated her unique abilities. In *The Actress of All Work,* she took on seven different roles in rapid succession. The piece had always been a favorite of audiences, since it showcased the quick-change talents of the star. The *Daily Alta California* reported:

> As the country girl she was inimitable, and kept the house in a perfect roar. As the high spirited actress she was equally perfect, and the old woman was garrulous and crack-voiced to the life. Then as the French *danseuse* she showed that grace and agility which is often wanting in many of those whose only merit is in their dancing, and who yet are accounted as great attractions at a theater.

Since Lola Montez had lately displayed her talents as a dancer in San Francisco, that veiled barb may have been aimed in the flamboyant Lola's direction.

Still, the Chapmans and Lola Montez occasionally played the same bill, and Lola, despite her reputation for horsewhipping editors who disparaged her talents, seemed to ignore Dr. Robinson's spoof of her dancing. Members of the public, however, sometimes came to Lola's defense. It was left to a gentleman admirer to defend Lola's honor and chastise Caroline in the *Herald.* At the end of his impassioned plea to remember the generosity of Lola Montez and cease attending the lampoon by Dr. Robinson as performed by the Chapmans, the writer reminded Caroline of her true calling:

> There probably never was, and never will be, an actress in San Francisco who has made more warm friends and admirers than Miss Caroline Chapman. She can play anything and do it well, and her name is an unfailing source of attraction wherever she appears. No matter what she undertakes, she renders herself acceptable and generally far more than

acceptable to her audience. If she were to "play the Devil," I haven't the least doubt she would do it perfectly, and be greeted with roars of applause; but we don't want to see any such character. Miss Chapman is a lady, and a most admirable artist; and I cannot believe that lowering her in this manner to a more profound depth than I had supposed low comedy to be capable of, can be any more agreeable to herself than it is to her admirers.

The writer went on to beg Caroline to spurn the mockery of Lola Montez:

No! no! We've had enough of this; personalities may amuse for a moment, but a little reflection makes them offensive. Give us "BEAUTY" again, charming Carry, and don't let them make a Mule of you any longer.

"Charming Carry" apparently ignored the request and by December 1853 was once again portraying a counterfeit "Countess" and keeping the audience in an uproar at the American Theatre.

Caroline and Uncle Billy and other family members rented a large house atop one of San Francisco's fabled hills, and there they laughed and partied with friends and fellow thespians. Yet no breath of scandal about the popular actress was ever published in the newspapers in the city.

On New Year's Day in 1862, another, and very surprising, notice appeared in the *Herald*. Under the headline "Elopement and Marriage," it was reported that Caroline Chapman had failed to appear onstage at the National Theatre to "take her part in the piece." The newspaper reported "the fair one could not be found." A Reverend Mr. Briggs reportedly married Caroline to a Mr. Nichols, "well and favorably known in San Francisco." The story indicated Caroline's father had not approved of the match. There is at least one incorrect fact in the report. William Chapman Sr., who claimed Caroline as his daughter, had died in the 1840s, and the man some say was actually her father, "Uncle Billy" Chapman, died in 1857. No more is heard about Mr. Nichols, the groom, but Caroline continued to attract attention as an actress of considerable talent. Her career, however, slowly dwindled as the City by the Bay became enthralled with a variety of entertainment from melodeons (saloons with music-hall entertainment, which included comedy, dance, and musical revues) to blackface minstrels to grand opera.

Caroline Chapman faded from the limelight as new, young actresses took to the boards in the vibrant city of San Francisco. By 1870 she was no longer performing. Perhaps it was the nature of the city, with its rapidly growing but transient population, that contributed to her descent into obscurity. Although the city had affectionately called her "Our Caroline" not many years before, and newspapers had praised her for her modesty as well as her peerless skills as an actress, in the *Daily Alta California* her obituary noted only: "In this city, May 8th, Miss Caroline Chapman, from the City of London, aged 58 years."

Catherine Hayes

THE IRISH PRIMA DONNA

Catherine Hayes is here, delighting the people with her vocal powers, which if not of the highest order, are extremely attractive; besides which, she appears with the most unquestionable reputation—a character that is supported by her conduct and deportment here.

—Mining scout Henry Huntley, San Francisco, 1852

A demure ten year-old girl sat in front of a clear, blue river, half-hidden under a canopy of willow trees in a lush garden, singing. Her silvery-toned voice resonated across the water and filled the afternoon sky with a melancholy sound. Couples canoeing on the river paddled toward the song, halted their boats, and waited in the shadows of the trees, listening. No one said a word. Not even a whisper gave away their position to the unknowing girl. Indeed she didn't realize anyone was paying attention until she finished her tune and rapturous applause commenced. Thus was the romantic beginning of Kate Hayes's singing career.

When Catherine Hayes was born in July 1818 in Ireland, her mother, Mary, compared the child's features to those of a cherub. Her talent for singing like an angel was soon revealed.

Kate's father, Arthur, abandoned her and her sister when they were small children, leaving the family destitute; consequently, Kate and her sister were forced to go to work as soon as they were old enough. From the age of eight, Kate worked a

Dublin, James Mc Glashan 1850.

CATHERINE HAYES   1818–1861

variety of odd jobs, from caring for infants to scrubbing inn floors. At nineteen she found employment as an assistant to a charwoman. She sang as she cleaned the homes she worked in, and passersby who overheard her were astonished at her remarkable voice.

Bishop Edmond Knoxx of Limerick heard her singing as he was passing by one of the homes she was cleaning, and he proclaimed that Kate had the most beautiful voice he had ever heard. He was the first to recognize her potential and consequently took her on as his protégé. He consulted with friends and helped raise the necessary funds to send Kate off to Dublin with letters of introduction to the accomplished vocalist and voice teacher Professor Antonio Sapio.

Professor Sapio agreed to train the young girl, as her voice possessed a clearness and mellowness he had rarely heard before. One month after her arrival in Dublin, Kate made her first formal public appearance at a concert hosted by her instructor. The discriminating audience was impressed by her talent, and the reviews in the newspaper the following day reflected the crowd's pleasure. But Sapio knew his protégé required more specialized training than he could provide and encouraged Catherine to continue her studies in France.

Bearing a letter of introduction from celebrated pianist George Osborne, Kate arrived in Paris in October of 1844. Manuel García, a renowned voice instructor who also taught other singers such as Jenny Lind, Maria Malibran, and Henriette Sontag, became her vocal teacher.

García taught Kate everything he could, then sent her to Italy to study for a career in opera. She concentrated on language arts and drama. In Milan, she met many influential theater patrons who arranged for her to audition for Guiseppe Provini, manager of the Italian Opera in Marseilles, France. Provini was so taken by her talent that he scheduled her operatic debut on May 10, 1845, as Elvira in Bellini's opera *I Puritani.*

At the end of Kate's first performance, the audience members leapt to their feet and bouquets of flowers filled the stage. Kate followed up her debut with another stunning performance, this time in Rossini's *Moses in Egypt*.

From France she traveled to Venice, where she appeared in *Lucia di Lammermoor*. Opera lovers were enraptured by the songbird. A theater critic with the *Venetian Journal* pronounced her the "greatest living prima Donna."

In 1845 she appeared at La Scala in Milan, where she sang the title role in Donizetti's *Linda di Chamounix*. Her performances in France, Venice, and Milan established her supremacy as an interpreter of Italian opera.

Now one of the most sought-after vocalists of Italian opera, "La Hayes," as her Italian fans referred to her, brought her talents to the United States early in 1851. She performed first in New York, then made the trek west to California. Theatergoers in San Francisco, anxious to see her, flooded into the American Theater Opera House. The lobby was magnificently decorated in gold and purple fabric for her performances. In 1852 *Far West News* reviewed her debut in *Le Prophète* in California:

> Her debut has been looked forward to with considerable anxiety, both on the part of those who accompanied the fair artist to these distant shores from the theaters of her achievements in the east, and by our citizens, to whom she is introduced crowned with honors, which even "the Lind" [opera singer Jenny Lind] might envy. . . .
>
> To say that the American Theater was filled would only be to confirm the expectation of every one who has heard of Catherine Hayes. The house had been re-arranged and put in excellent order for the reception of so large a company. . . . Several minutes before the opening of the concert, all the vacant places in the dress circle and parquette were filled, and one of the most intelligent and respectable audiences ever assembled within the walls of a theater in this city awaited the appearance of the star of the evening.
>
> Long and loud were the cheers and applause, which

greeted her entrée. She acknowledged again and again the enthusiastic testimonial, and again and again the audience cheered and applauded. Silence having been restored, Miss Hayes sang the sweet plaintive invocation, the "Ah mon fils," (translated means "Ah, my son,") one of the most touching gems of Meyerbeer's music. It was while standing at the foot-lights, amid the storm of applause, that our citizens had the first view of Miss Catherine Hayes. . . . Miss Hayes is about thirty years of age. She is a graceful, queen-like person, of medium stature, with a fair oval face. Her features are regular, hair bright auburn, eyes blue, and her face wears an intellectual expression without much animation. She dresses with taste, and her manner is perfectly easy and self-possessed; her gesticulation appropriate and graceful.

Catherine Hayes gave forty-two performances at the American Theater, playing each time to a standing-room-only crowd. Tickets for the best seats in the house were auctioned off for $1,125. She was one of the greatest sensations to hit the frontier.

At the close of each of her shows, hundreds of bouquets were thrown from audience members onto the stage. Occasionally those bouquets contained gold pieces, but not everyone could afford such expensive displays of admiration. So enchanted was one miner by the singer's voice (a man who no doubt spent all he had to see her perform) that he tossed his ragged hat onto the stage and cried out, "By the powers! Darling, here's my hat fer yer, and it's all I have got to give ye!"

In February of 1853 Kate traveled to Sacramento to give a concert at the local Presbyterian church. Seats for this performance were sold at auction as well, and Captain John Sutter secured a ticket for $1,200. Author Constance Rourke attended Kate's February 8 performance and made note of how proudly Captain Sutter carried himself into the theater. He was thrilled to own the ticket for the best seat in the house. "The stout, affable old man made a conspicuous entry with a detachment of officers to the sound of thunderous applause," wrote Rourke, "and was seated with ceremony in the front row on an opulent and spacious green plush sofa."

Kate began that particular program by serenading the enthusiastic crowd with Irish ballads she'd composed herself. Later, William Michael O'Rourke, a violinist, and Monsieur Chenal, master of the clarinet, performed. Kate concluded the evening with a tearful rendition of "Home Sweet Home."

Kate ended her tour of California's Gold Country on April 18, 1853. One of her farewell recitals was held in the Alta in Grass Valley. Hundreds of people were in attendance. A glowing review of her performance appeared in the *Nevada Journal*:

> The voice of the cantatrice broke forth in notes of most bewitching sweetness and harmony. The excitement of the audience increased to a furious extent, no doubt with proud ratification that they had heard for once in their lives, the voice that had awakened the admiration of the western world.

Kate delighted the citizens of Grass Valley and nearby Nevada City with her genteel demeanor and elegant style. She visited many sites in the mining towns, including a few working gold mines, and even tried panning for nuggets in one of the streams. So admired was Kate Hayes by the residents of Grass Valley that they named a street after her.

After leaving Grass Valley, Kate gave one last performance in San Francisco before boarding a steamer that would take her to Chile. A review of the San Francisco show appeared in the *Daily Alta California* on April 30, 1853:

> We've seldom seen in San Francisco a finer audience than were assembled in San Francisco Hall last evening to hear Miss Hayes' last concert. The house was very full, and the

walls were decorated by a line of unfortunate gentlemen who could not obtain seats. Miss Hayes was in excellent voice, no doubt inspired by the full house, and perhaps desirous of leaving a pleasant impression during her absence.

On October 8, 1857, Kate married her longtime agent, William Bushell; unfortunately, he died the following July of heart failure. Catherine died from a stroke a few years later. Her estate was estimated at more than a quarter million dollars.

Her contribution to the art of opera is invaluable, and she played a significant role in the development of the music and culture of frontier California. One theater critic likened her talent to a "prize of abundant worth." The *Honolulu Argus* wrote that she "could charm a soul from purgatory. In a word, she is a living Aeolian harp, tuned by the Almighty and not to be beat."

Matilda Heron

STAR OF THE AMERICAN THEATER

Never have we seen a popular enthusiasm more fervid and unremitting than what Miss Heron has created. Night after night her houses have not only been filled, but crowded and the ardent thousands who have contributed to her applause seem to have been governed by a feeling of direct and active personal interest in her welfare.

—*California Chronicle*, San Francisco, January 30, 1854

The American Theater in San Francisco stood patiently waiting for patrons to fill its empty hall. The building was a simple structure with a moderate-sized stage and kerosene footlights. It had played host to many of the aspiring entertainers of the early Gold Rush days. At one time its seats had been filled to capacity every night, but now times had changed. The new Metropolitan Theater, billed as "the most gorgeous theater in the United States," was attracting the clientele that had previously flocked to the American. It would take an incredible talent to save the playhouse now. It was late December 1853, and the managers of the American were making plans to close down the hall.

Actor James Murdock convinced them to keep the doors open for a performance from a thespian he had worked with in Boston—a show for whomever would attend.

On Monday, December 26, Matilda Heron, a very young and not yet cele-

MATILDA HERON 1830–1877

brated actress, stepped out onto the American Theater stage and instantly captured the hearts of the audience seated before her. She portrayed the character Bianca from the play *Fazio* and transported the crowd to another place and time with her talent.

By the end of the week, she was playing to a full house every night, resuscitating the expiring American and halting the theater's early demise. Critics proclaimed that her success lay in "her perfect naturalness of manner, the total absence of those screamings, rantings, and gesticulations which have grown up rank and deep-rooted weeds on the dramatic field!" Four weeks after her arrival in the West, Matilda had become the star she'd always dreamed of being.

Matilda Agnes Heron was born on December 1, 1830, in Londonderry, Ireland. Her parents were John Heron and Mary Laughlin Heron, and she was the youngest of five children, all of whom were educated in private schools. Shortly after she turned twelve, her father moved the family to Philadelphia, Pennsylvania, where he prospered as a merchant. His income allowed him to send Matilda to a French academy. There, influenced by one of her teachers, she developed an interest in the theater.

Matilda's first efforts in the arts were in the fields of poetry and literature. She was successful to a fair extent, but the praise she received was not prompt or palpable enough for her practical and ardent mind. She felt the stage was a more fitting challenge and decided to pursue acting as her profession, against the wishes of her fiercely religious parents, who believed actors were in a league with the devil himself. For three years she studied under master thespian Peter Richings in "the private philosophy of the stage."

As soon as she had completed her studies, she stepped onto the stage of the Walnut Theater in Philadelphia. It was 1851, and every noteworthy actor and actress of the time had played the Walnut. Dignitaries, including presidents, attended shows there. Audiences were awed by her performance in the play *Camille*. She possessed a grace and ease that many of her fellow thespians admired. According to reviews of the time, her performances were "loaded with emotional intensity."

Talent agent George Lewis was quick to recognize her potential and convinced her to let him be her representative. George believed she could earn a great deal of money performing for entertainment-starved miners in California. Two years after her debut in Philadelphia, she and George Lewis were on their way to San Francisco by steamer.

The ocean voyage west, however, was a tragic one. George became ill along the way and died six days before their inbound steamer docked on December 25, 1853. Matilda was alone, and her arrival went unnoticed. Just before she was scheduled to board another steamer to take her back east, she met up with James Murdock, a noted tragedian with whom she had worked in the past. If not for him, her career in California would never have started. Learning of her plight and attesting to her talents, Murdoch convinced the owners of the American Theater to let Matilda perform there.

Frank Soule of the *California Chronicle* marveled at the audience's response to her performance on opening night:

> Nevertheless, on the night of the 26th of December, the American Theater was thrilled to host the friendless candidate's performance. A burst of welcome greeted her entrance, and then the house subsided into a state of nervous anxiety, such as, perhaps, was never felt before, for a person so entirely unknown. She spoke; a profound silence followed, which showed that every mind was working on her merits; she spoke again, and a breath of satisfaction and relief could be audibly distinguished. At length the process of the piece brought her to one of those points which enable her to show, in pathos, the deep harmonious music of the soul, and then burst forth a cheer that made the building shake. Suspense was over; she was received into the innermost appreciation of her audience, and all concern for her future success, by those

who had assumed the responsibility of an opinion in advance, was lost in an enthusiasm that knew no bounds. Her triumph was not confined to the front; even the actresses embraced and kissed her, and she was equally petted before and behind the curtain.

Summing up her successful engagement, Soule wrote:

> She has played twelve nights in the test characters of the tragic drama, and after a success unparalleled, closed with a reputation which places her at the very pinnacle of fame. . . . Genius alone can excite such a sentiment as this, and they who win it have reason to thank Heaven, for they are the favored of the gods.

Historian John H. McCabe wrote often of Matilda's extraordinary talent and generosity. His unpublished theatrical journal notes that on December 30, 1854, Matilda donated the proceeds from her performance to her agent's widow. She insisted that the money be sent back to Mrs. Lewis by the next steamer bound for the East. McCabe writes that many were impressed by Matilda's gift and were anxious to reward her for showing such kindness:

> This noble conduct, struck from the soul under circumstances which forbids all suspicion of artifice, became known through members of the company, and before night a number of gentlemen spontaneously contributed to the purchase of a diamond cross for the generous girl, as an appropriate reward of an act of such pious and munificent charity.

Reporter Frank Soule, on hand the evening the diamond cross was presented to the adored actress, was equally moved:

We do not recollect ever to have beheld a scene of equal excitement in a theater to the one exhibited during the presentation of that jewel. Ignorant of what was to be said or done (for the whole arrangement was but a few hours old), Miss Heron was called before the curtain with the theater manager. The whole house rose, and her arrival at the center of the stage was the signal for a shower of bouquets, too numerous to be gathered, which literally deluged her feet. "What will she do with them all?" said a voice during a momentary lull. "She'll walk upon them!" was the answer of a dozen, and three cheers endorsed the sentiment.

At this moment a large and magnificent bunch of flowers was handed by a gentleman from the crowded corner of the orchestra, on the top of which glittered the sparkling present, and beside it a note which the theater manager was requested to read.

"Dear Young Lady—A few among the thousands whom your merits have already made your friends in California desire to present you this small evidence of their esteem. It is a symbol of the religion you profess, and we trust that while it reminds you of your faith, it will at the same time be received as a pledge that genius never can be friendless on these shores."

Many emotions crossed Matilda's face as she listened to the words. She laughed, cried, and then made a short speech thanking the gentlemen for their kindness, after which she "was lodged firmly in the hearts of that transported audience . . . so that 'six yoke of oxen could not drag her out,'" according to the *Chronicle*.

The proceeds from the evening's benefit came to more than $1,600. At the end of Matilda's first week at the American, management presented her with an extra $500 as an acknowledgment of her role in keeping the theater open against the formidable attractions of the competing Metropolitan.

Matilda's run at the American Theater included stellar performances in such shows as *The Countess of Love, The Wife, Love's Sacrifice, The Honeymoon,* and *The Stranger.* One local reviewer confessed that he had been so moved by Miss Heron's representation of Mrs. Haller in *The Stranger* that "he would never dare to undergo the ordeal of seeing a repetition of that performance."

A reporter for the *San Francisco Evening Bulletin* had lavish praise for her performance as Juliana in *The Honeymoon:*

> Throughout the changes of that metamorphosis she was true to nature and to reason. The natural vanities of the giddy girl, her ambition of the coronet, her indignation when convinced of the deception practiced upon her, her resistance to the authority of her husband, her deception to regain her freedom and divorce, the gradual change wrought by love and association, and the full gush of love at last, with the delight of gratified pride which comes as a crown to love, and her own reformation in temper and manner, were all given with a truthfulness to nature that carried everything before it, no less the hearts than the heads of the audience.

Matilda Heron finished her opening season in Gold Rush Country to great fanfare. Frank Soule summed up her California triumph:

> A debut among strangers, without prestige—twelve remarkable performances—two occasions when the sale of tickets was stopped in the afternoon—and a benefit at the conclusion, when, despite storms, the counter attractions of a grand oratorio at Musical Hall, and an imposing military display at the Metropolitan, she, on the short notice of a day, drew a densely crowded house. She has therefore won

every description of endorsement, as well from actors as from the public and the press, and she stands a fixed dramatic identity; a dazzling star, whose radiance will always shine preeminent, by whatever constellation it may be surrounded.

During her stay in San Francisco, Matilda met Henry H. Byrne, a handsome, prominent attorney with the Mission Dolores law firm. In June of 1854 the two were secretly married in a private ceremony, and, according to the custom of the day, Matilda retired from the theater. She longed for the footlights, however, and returned to acting three weeks later, an action that so horrified her new husband that they separated.

Humiliated and heartbroken, Matilda left California and headed back to Philadelphia. She joined a prestigious acting troupe and traveled to Washington, Chicago, and New York. Along the way she perfected her portrayal of Camille in the play of the same name, prompting theater critics across the country to proclaim her "the most sensational Camille in America."

In December 1857 Matilda entered into a second marriage, this time with conductor and composer Robert Stoepel. The two had a daughter they named Helene. The marriage was not a happy one, and Matilda sought refuge in her work, traveling again with the Philadelphia-based acting troupe, with her daughter by her side. She returned to California in 1865. This time the rave reviews were not only for her performances but for her daughter's as well. Seven-year-old Helene performed under the stage name Bijou Heron and was called a brilliant singer and actress.

Matilda and Robert Stoepel divorced in 1869. She lost herself in her work again, taking time to write, produce, and star in her own plays. She created a sensation wherever she performed. Her acting style was unique, as she followed her feelings rather than the rules of elocution, eschewing the use of grand gestures and booming variations of the voice. She hypnotized audiences and critics alike with her dark, flashing eyes, which transformed her otherwise plain face.

By the early 1870s her health was failing. Her once slender figure grew corpulent, and her rich dark hair turned gray. Her popularity began to wane. She had to supplement her dwindling income by teaching drama and stage performance.

Her last years were not happy ones. She acted some but was ill and impoverished. Over the course of her career, she had earned more than $200,000 dollars playing Camille alone. Now, at the age of forty-two, she was broke, having lost all her money to extravagant living and lavish generosity. On January 17, 1872, a benefit was held for her in New York. A total of $4,000 was raised to help sustain the actress.

She ended her acting career on the same stage on which she'd begun it—the Walnut Theater in Philadelphia. During the 1874–75 season she portrayed an array of emotional characters, including Lady Macbeth. Her daughter, who by this time had established herself as a successful actress, was a constant source of happiness to her in her final years. (Helene later went on to marry the celebrated actor Henry Miller and became the mother of theatrical producer Gilbert Heron Miller.)

Early in 1877 Matilda's ill health necessitated an operation, from which she did not recover. She subsequently died at the age of forty-seven at her New York City home. Matilda was laid to rest in Greenwood Cemetery in Brooklyn. The "emotional" form of acting she developed is currently being taught at universities.

Lillie Langtry

THE JERSEY LILY

I resent Mrs. Langtry. She has no right to be intelligent, daring and independent as well as lovely. It is a frightening combination of attributes.

—George Bernard Shaw, June 12, 1884

The Royal Aquarium in Westminster, England, was a hub of activity on April 6, 1876. Many members of London's wealthy aristocratic society were on hand for the gala opening of the magnificent structure built entirely underwater.

Dignitaries, barristers, popular sculptors, artists, and photographers were there to witness the occasion and to be inspired by the colorful coral reefs, graceful marine life, and crystal-blue waters. Their attention, however, was drawn away from the oceanic scenery when a tall, curvaceous young woman with Titian red hair entered the room. She was adorned in a simple black gown, a gift from her doting parents. Her azure eyes scanned the faces staring back at her, and she smiled ever so slightly. Within moments of her arrival, visitors descended upon the woman to admire her beauty.

Eminent portrait painters and photographers approached the unassuming woman and asked her to sit for them. Poets sought introductions and then recited blank verse about her arresting features. By the end of the evening, Lillie Langtry was the toast of Great Britain—a Professional Beauty to be reckoned with.

Professional Beauties were highborn ladies, most of them married, who hap-

LILLIE LANGTRY   1853–1929

pened to be lovely and who enhanced their loveliness by dressing handsomely and indulging in exceptional grooming. Portraits of these Beauties were sold to enthusiastic followers. Pictures of Lillie Langtry would be no exception.

The night of the aquarium opening, Frank Mills, a pen-and-ink artist who illustrated for newspapers and magazines, drew two sketches of Lillie. He presented her with one of the sketches and reproduced the second. It was the first portrait of the actress to appear in shops, and it was available to the general public for a penny.

Emile Charlotte LeBreton was born to William Corbet and Emilie Martin LeBreton in October of 1853 on the Isle of Jersey, a few miles off the coast of Saint-Malo, France. She was the only daughter in a family of six children. Her mother called her "Lillie," which fit the beautiful child with lily-white skin.

Family recollections, including her own, indicate that she was a tomboy from the time she first learned to walk. She competed in games and exercises with her brothers, climbed cliffs, swam, and was an expert bareback rider by the time she was six. In her autobiography, *The Days I Knew*, she credits her brothers with influencing her and making her childhood a joyful time: "Living the life of my brothers transformed me into an incorrigible tomboy. I could climb trees and vault fences with the best of them, and I entered with infinite relish into their practical jokes. We laughed for hours at the harmless, mischievous fun we always created."

By the time she was fifteen, the irrepressible tomboy had grown into quite a beauty. Soldiers from the Royal Army started to take notice of her lovely face and mature figure. A twenty-three-year-old lieutenant posted to the Jersey garrison fell in love with Lillie on sight and proposed to marry her. When her age was revealed, the soldier was stunned, for he had mistaken her for being much older.

Lillie soon abandoned tree-climbing and began to read the classics and work with tutors. During a trip to London, she learned many of the social arts while mixing with England's high society. In the evenings she read the plays of William Shakespeare and Ben Jonson aloud to her father. "Between the ages of sixteen and twenty," she wrote of herself, "I learned the magic of words, the beauty and excitement of poetic imagery. I learned there was something in life other than horses, climbing cliffs, the sea and the long Jersey tides."

When she returned to the Isle of Jersey, Lillie became convinced that there was no future for her there and dreamt of leaving, just as her five brothers had. She had no training of any sort for a profession as she had been reared to become the wife of a gentleman. She knew marriage would be her only form of escape.

Soon after Lillie's twentieth birthday, she met the man she would marry. A storm at sea forced a large yacht from England into the Jersey harbor. Edward Langtry, the owner of the beautiful ship, was a dashing young man with dark hair and black eyes, and he strutted in his handsomely tailored clothes. Lillie set her sights on the handsome man and his wealth. "One day there came into the harbor a most beautiful yacht. I met the owner and fell in love with the yacht. To become the mistress of the yacht, I married the owner," wrote Lillie in *The Days I Knew*.

Edward fell in love with Lillie, and the two were married on March 9, 1874. The couple sailed for London aboard Edward's ship, *The Red Gauntlet*. The two lived on the yacht for nine months, rubbing elbows with some of England's most renowned aristocrats. The pair ended their honeymoon cruise in the autumn of 1874 and moved into a mansion called The Cliff Lodge in Southampton. Lillie quickly became bored with the provincial life in Southampton and convinced Edward to sell the house and its furnishings and relocate to London.

Lillie's favorite part of living in London was attending the shows at all the various theaters. After seeing performances of *Hamlet* and *The Merchant of Venice*, she was "thrilled beyond my powers to describe my feelings." The recollections of those experiences later would persuade her to pursue an acting career.

Within two years of moving to London, Lillie Langtry was the toast of the town. Her Professional Beauty status brought about a steady succession of invitations to the dinners and balls of British royalty and elite. Lillie's rise in popularity pushed Edward into the background of her life. Uncomfortable with the attention his beautiful wife was receiving and at her increasing indifference toward him, he

Known initially for her beauty, Lillie embarked on a theater career on the advice of her friend Oscar Wilde.

drowned his troubles in expensive wine and champagne.

Beauty alone was responsible for Lillie Langtry's initial renown. Her photographs were printed in French and American newspapers, and by the time she was twenty-seven she was famous in those countries, as well. It wasn't until a few years later, however, when Edward had lost his fortune due to mismanagement and extravagant living, that Lillie considered the notion of capitalizing on her popularity by becoming an actress.

The writer Oscar Wilde, whom Lillie had met at society parties, convinced her that the theater was her calling. He told her that "she would be mad if she contemplated any career other than the stage." Wilde argued that audiences would flock to see the Professional Beauty in person.

The respected British actor Henry Irving offered Lillie a role in a new play set to open in the 1880–81 theatrical season. The part was small, but important. Lillie was considering it when she learned she was pregnant, so she declined the offer and retired from society, giving birth to a daughter in April 1881. She named the girl Jeanne Marie. Edward was out working at sea when Jeanne Marie was born, and she never told him they had a child together. Not long after Jeanne's birth, Lillie informed Edward that she was leaving him.

There was no time to grieve over the demise of her marriage. Lillie received offers from theater owners asking her to join their acting troupe. Knowing that they were attracted only by her beauty, she refused all offers, deciding instead to take acting lessons. Oscar Wilde introduced her to the critically acclaimed actress and teacher Henrietta Hodson Labouchère, who agreed to take Lillie on as her pupil and train her as a thespian. After months of intense study and preparation, Lillie took to the stage for the first time on December 15, 1881, portraying Kate Hardcastle in *She Stoops to Conquer* at the Theatre Royal.

The theater was filled to capacity, and audience members included the Prince and Princess of Wales as well as representatives of the domestic and foreign press.

Reviews were complimentary: "Mrs. Langtry was not only lovely, which we expected, but surprised us by displaying potential as an actress," wrote the *London Times*; "She will become a star!" predicted *The Daily Telegraph*.

Theater managers again clamored for a chance to star the famous beauty in one of their shows. Henrietta Labouchère, now Lillie's manager, secured positions for Lillie at only the most prestigious playhouses. She toured London and Scotland, performing for full houses nightly and earning 250 pounds a night for her efforts. Even bigger earnings were on the horizon.

New York theater owner and producer Henry Abbey saw Lillie in a show in Edinburgh and was instantly captivated by her talent. He wrote Henrietta with a generous proposal for Lillie, including an offer of 50 percent of the gross proceeds from her shows. Henrietta encouraged her pupil to accept, but Lillie held out for 65 percent of the gross and payment of all her travel expenses. After several days of haggling, the producer gave in. Henry Abbey wrote, "Mrs. Langtry is as tough a business woman as she is a lovely lady. She may smell of delicious perfume, but nothing creases her hide except dollar bills."

Before embarking on her U.S. tour, Lillie used her strong business sense to negotiate a contract with the Pear's Soap Company and thus became the first woman to endorse a commercial product. She was paid 132 pounds to sign a statement that she owed her flawless skin to regular use of Pear's Soap. Her bank account and popularity grew, and she endorsed other products, such as Brown's Iron Bitters.

She set sail for America with assurance from her manager and producer that if she were successful in the United States, she could earn as much as a quarter of a million dollars on her first tour alone. Lillie's friend Oscar Wilde was on hand to meet her when she arrived in America. The day before he was to greet her he told a newspaper reporter how much she meant to him: "I would rather have discovered Mrs. Langtry than to have discovered America. You have asked whether she is indeed a beauty, and I can reply to such nonsense only by saying that you will see for yourself. No, I will go farther. She is the most beautiful woman in all the world, and will be a beauty still at eighty-five. It was for such as she that Troy was destroyed, and well it might have been."

Several newspaper reporters awaited Lillie's arrival so that they could "see for themselves" this actress of such high praise. They were not disappointed. Lillie dressed for the occasion in a figure-hugging dark-blue dress. Her graciousness, beauty, and charm overwhelmed the press.

Lillie Langtry was a huge success in New York. Clothing, alcoholic beverages, and dry goods were named for her. Songs and special waltzes were written for her. Her tour ended in March 1883, and she went back to England as one of the wealthiest actresses of that time. Her return met with great fanfare in London. She received royal receptions everywhere she went. She enjoyed a visit with her daughter, Jeanne (who she referred to as her niece in public), and spent time with her parents.

To hone her acting skills, she then enrolled in an art conservatory and took instruction from the leading dramatic teacher of the time, Joseph Regnier. Lillie was dedicated to learning all she could about the acting trade—determined to win recognition for more than her beauty.

In April 1886 she decided to tour the United States again, this time from the Atlantic to the Pacific and back again. She traveled in a private railroad car designed especially for her by William Mann, the inventor and manufacturer of the sleeping car. She named the magnificently decorated car the Lalee, an East Indian word meaning "flirt."

Lillie arrived in San Francisco in July 1887. She was awestruck by the City by the Bay and purchased a 4,000-acre ranch with plans to retire there. She was so fascinated with America as a whole that she renounced her British allegiance and applied for naturalization as a citizen of the United States.

Lillie captivated audiences across California with performances in *As in a Looking Glass* and *Anthony and Cleopatra*. Newspapers throughout California's Gold Country hailed her work as "superb," and theatergoers would withstand any hard-

ship to see the actress perform. During her time in the West, she was the chief subject of discussion among miners, socialites, and critics. "Langtry is the topic just
now," wrote the *San Francisco Call* on June 26, 1887:

> From the different points where she played during her
> progress across the continent, carefully prepared booms have
> preceded her to this city, until the last sharp, short shot was
> fired from Oakland, where she performed last evening. The
> interior papers have indulged odd vagaries in regard to the
> lady, preferring in some cases to criticize the actress from a
> physical aspect rather than to discuss her mental require
> ments.
>
> A Stockton paper, for instance, gives the measurements
> of the Lily's figure, including her limbs in detail, with the
> precision of a knight of the shears taking dimensions for a
> suit of tailor made clothing, a luxury which ladies indulge in
> occasionally, to the disgust of dress-makers of their own sex.
>
> It is of record too, that the heat wave, while she was in
> Sacramento, did not improve the temper of this favored
> child of fortune, and she rather snubbed the Sacramentans,
> who were a little tardy to welcome her at the theater. She did
> not consider what the lovers of art resident in the River City
> had to face: Two dollars per ticket and one hundred and fif-
> teen degree heat in the shade. She must be artiste, indeed,
> who could draw a full house under such circumstances.

Her acting skills and beauty weren't the only aspect of her life that caused discussion among patrons of the arts. Lillie's personal life at times almost overshadowed
her stage work. While in California, she finally acquired a divorce from Edward
Langtry. He never got over losing Lillie. Rumors of the numerous affairs she had prior
to the dissolution of their marriage contributed to his mental illness. He was eventually declared insane and died at the Cheshire County Asylum on October 3, 1897.

The Jersey Lily (a nickname she acquired because of where she was born) was romantically linked to the Prince of Wales, gambler Diamond Jim Brady, and actor Maurice Barrymore. Everywhere she went men found her shockingly attractive. Among her famous admirers was Judge Roy Bean of Texas. Bean instantly fell in love with Lillie after seeing her photograph posted on a playbill. Soon the walls of Judge Bean's saloon courthouse in Vinegaroon, Texas, were covered with her pictures and press clippings. He renamed that town Langtry, and Lillie visited the town named in her honor in 1904. Judge Bean had died not long before. She toured his Jersey Lily Saloon and drank a toast in his honor. Langtry residents gave her Bean's pet bear, which had been chained for years to the foot of his bed, and the animal ran off as soon as it was released. Lillie was then presented with the Judge's revolver, the same one he'd used to keep order in his court.

Lillie's transcontinental tour included performances in some of Nevada's richest silver towns. Virginia City miners rolled out a red carpet for the actress and welcomed her train with cheers and applause.

One of the town's most notable residents, Mark Twain, was quite taken with Lillie. During her stay in Virginia City, the two met on a number of occasions. He was impressed with her dramatic ability and what he called "her clarity of judgment." He wrote:

> Contrary to what one would expect of a woman whose fame was based on her beauty, Mrs. Langtry is an exceptionally intelligent person. She must read constantly because she is able to discuss in detail any book, classical or modern, English or American or French, that is mentioned for her. I know she isn't shamming, because I questioned her in some detail, and she KNEW the books. She also reads the newspapers, and doesn't bother with the trivia. She can talk about world affairs or financial matters or whatever with the good sense one would expect of a man who keeps up to date.

She meets a stranger as an equal, and although she's so pretty her beauty is blinding, she doesn't rely on feminine charm. She's what she is, and she expects one to take her or leave her. She is good company with her friends, but it would be hell to be married to her. She's too damn bright.

Everywhere Lillie performed across the West, she packed venues and received excellent reviews. She ended her American tour back in New York. She was now recognized as an accomplished thespian, and her talents were sought after by some of the most prominent playwrights of the day. Richard Mansfield, Haddam Chambers, and Oscar Wilde all wrote pieces especially for her. She went back to Europe in late 1892 but returned to the United States in 1894, in great demand to star in several shows all over the country.

Articles about her scandalous romantic affairs appeared in newspapers and magazines alongside the complimentary reviews she received for her work. The enormous amount of attention paid to her love life never harmed her professional standing; if anything, it created longer lines at the box office. Rumors of her romantic liaison with wealthy Cuban Antonio Terry brought out curious fans in droves. Terry's wife, young opera star Sibyl Sanderson, had heard about the rumored relationship, and she cut short her own theatrical tour to travel to New York to confront Lillie. Theatergoers believed she would do so at one of Lillie's programs. No one wanted to miss that show. However, Sibyl and Lillie never faced off at the theater—or anywhere else. Considering her reputation to be marred by the rumored affair, Sibyl divorced Antonio.

At times Lillie's theatrical performances were upstaged by her beautiful costumes and dazzling jewelry. Critics claimed the clothing and gems made audiences forget the play, whereas Lillie maintained that "sometimes diamonds were needed to bolster the material." Thousands of women bought seats in the hope that they would attend a performance in which Lillie wore her fabulous gems.

After another extended trip across the ocean to visit her family on the Isle of Jersey and to perform for the Queen of England, Lillie answered the call of the American public and returned to her adopted country in 1902, when she was fifty-one years old. Before she returned the press speculated on whether or not her beauty had faded in the years she had been away. The seventy-five reporters and photographers who came out to meet her ship as it pulled into New York Harbor were stunned. Lillie greeted them on the ship's deck, attired in an ermine-trimmed coat of sable. She had never been lovelier; the actress looked as though she had not aged a day.

The *New York Sun* described her:

> Mrs. Langtry should be renamed Ponce de Leon, but on second thought he should have been called Lillie Langtry. He searched for the Fountain of Youth, but it was obvious to all who greeted her on board the ship, as it soon will be obvious to all New York, that she found it. One would be lacking in gallantry to beauty if one revealed her true age, so let it suffice that she looks half her years.

Not long after her arrival in the States, Lillie was flooded with offers from magazine, book, and newspaper publishers to write her life story. William Randolph Hearst was immensely interested in seeing the story of Lillie Langtry in print. Though the bidding was intense, the actress turned down all book offers, saying that the "time wasn't right." Not until late in her life did she finally pen her autobiography, doing so without a ghostwriter. The book, entitled *The Days I Knew*, was published in 1925.

In 1904 Lillie made her final sweep through the American West. Her performance in the witty English comedy *Mrs. Deering's Divorce* at the Columbia Theater in San Francisco was well received, and critics applauded her talent and sustained beauty. According to the *San Francisco Chronicle:*

> Mrs. Langtry has not lost in the many years since we saw her, her personal attraction. An opera glass fixed on her may possibly show some traces of the years, but the face is still handsome, the head has yet a beautiful poise, and altogether Mrs. Langtry is not in any material way less interesting than before. One cannot call her matronly yet. The natural graces of the society belle give her the old distinction, and she is very much more at ease with her acting than she used to be.

After touring in a pair of critically and financially successful plays and fully enjoying vaudeville life, Lillie announced her intention to retire from the stage. In 1919 she gave up the theater, moved to a new home in Monaco, and plunged into the social whirl of the Riviera's permanent residents. Her daughter and four grandchildren spent time with her there.

World-famous Lillie Langtry took ill in the fall of 1928. Her ailment was diagnosed as bronchitis, complicated by pleurisy. She never completely recovered, and her weakened lungs were attacked again by a case of influenza. The actress died on February 12, 1929. She was seventy-six years old. She was buried next to her parents on the Isle of Jersey in the churchyard of St. Saviour's.

News of her death spread quickly throughout the United States. The front pages of newspapers across America recalled her contributions to the theater, and some editorials declared her passing as "an era that has come to an end."

Adah Menken

THE FRENZY OF FRISCO

A striking picture, it was far out of the common run in that day: a head of Byronic mold; a fair, proud throat, quite open to admiration, for the sailor collar that might have graced the wardrobe of the Poet-Lord was carelessly knotted upon the bosom with a voluminously flowing silk tie. The hair, black, glossy, short and curly, gave to the head, forehead and nape of the neck a half-feminine masculinity suggestive of the Apollo Belvedere.

— Poet Charles Warren Stoddard's description of Adah Menken's portrait on display at San Francisco's Maguire Opera House in July 1863

On August 24, 1863, San Francisco's elite flocked to Maguire's Opera House. Ladies in diamonds and furs rode up in handsome carriages; gentlemen in opera capes and silk hats strutted in stylishly. It was an opening night such as the city had never before seen. All one thousand seats in the theater were filled with curious spectators anxious to see the celebrated melodramatic actress Adah Menken perform.

Adah was starring in the role that made her famous, that of Prince Ivan in *Mazeppa*. It was rumored that she preferred to play the part in the nude. Newspapers in the East reported that audiences found the scantily clad thespian's act "shocking, scandalous, horrifying and even delightful." The story line of the play was taken from a Byron poem in which a Tartar prince is condemned to ride forever in the

ADAH MENKEN   1835–1868

desert stripped naked and lashed to a fiery, untamed steed. Adah insisted on playing the part as true to life as possible.

The audience waited with bated breath for Adah to walk out onto the stage,
and when she did, a hush fell over the crowd. She was beautiful, possessing curly, dark
hair and big, dark eyes. Adorned in a flesh-colored body nylon and tight-fitting
underwear, she left the audience speechless. During the play's climactic scene, supporting characters strapped the star to the back of a black stallion. The horse raced
up the narrow runway between cardboard mountain crags. The audience responded
with thunderous applause. Adah Menken had captured the heart of another city in
the West.

Adah Isaacs Menken was born Adois Dolores McCord on June 15, 1835, in
New Orleans, Louisiana. Her mother was a very beautiful French Creole, and her
father was a highly respected free Negro. Prejudice against her ethnicity plagued her
early career. Theater owners who were familiar with her heritage refused to hire her. As
a result, Adah created many stories about her upbringing and parentage. Historians
believe this was necessary for her to secure work and be accepted by audiences across
the United States. The confusion about Adah's lineage added a hint of mystery to her
image. The truth about her roots was not uncovered until the early 1900s.

Adah's father died when she was seven. A few years after his death her mother
married Doctor J. C. Campbell, the chief surgeon of the U.S. Army. According to
biographies about Adah's life, Campbell was a generous man who encouraged the
talents of Adah and her sister. Adah was a gifted writer, painter, actor, and dancer.
By the time she was eleven, she was an accomplished artist, having published several
poems and danced in the ballet of the French Opera House in New Orleans. She
was exceedingly bright, and spoke French, Spanish, and Hebrew fluently.

Adah's stepfather died when she was thirteen, leaving her crushed, for she had
come to count on his encouragement and support in her acting aspirations. Adah's relationship with her mother was strained. She was jealous of the affection her husband
showed for Adah and thus treated her badly. In a letter to her sister dated July 1867,

Adah wrote about how her mother "disliked her" and how she dreamed of a better life.

Shortly after Doctor Campbell's death, Adah's mother took up company with a man who made improper advances toward her daughters. Adah left home when she could suffer it no longer. She joined a local troupe of entertainers and traveled to Havana, Cuba, to dance for political figures and foreign dignitaries. She was well received and called "The Queen of the Plaza." A fellow actor on tour with Adah at this time named Horace Keene wrote, "Scarcely 16, she overwhelmed the audience with her charm and talent. Her tiny frame, crisp black curls and dark, sparkling eyes made her a beauty unlike any that have entertained here before. Is it any wonder Havana is bewitched by her?"

All the applause and attention she received helped Adah forget her sorrow over the loss of her stepfather. The players in her troupe convinced her she could earn more money as an actress than as a dancer. When she returned to the United States, she abandoned ballet and turned to acting.

The young girl began her quest for stardom in Liberty, Texas. She made a living giving public readings of Shakespeare's works, writing newspaper articles and poems, and teaching dance classes. She began to search for a rich husband to support her acting career by placing an advertisement in the *Liberty Gazette* newspaper on November 23, 1855:

> I'm young and free, the pride of girls
> With hazel eyes and "nut brown curls"
> They say I'm not void of beauty—
> I love my friends and respect my duty—
> I've had full many a BEAU IDEAL,
> Yet never—never—found one real—
> There must be one I know somewhere,
> In all this circumambient air;
> And I should dearly love to see him!
> Now what if you should chance to be him?

Alexander Isaacs Menken, a well-to-do pit musician and conductor, was touring the Texas Panhandle when he came upon Adah's delightful poem. He wrote to her, and the two met, instantly firing one another with passion and ambition. They were married the following April in Galveston, Texas. Soon after Adah and Alexander said "I do," Adah began working onstage in supporting roles at the Liberty Shakespeare Theater and, with her husband's financial help, quickly moved on to lead roles at the Crescent Dramatic Association of New Orleans.

Alexander worshiped his new bride, and Adah was quite taken with him, but their notions of what married life should be were diametrically opposed. Alexander wanted a traditional, stay-at-home wife who would make his meals and raise his children. Adah was not at all interested in such a domestic life; in fact, in one of the articles she wrote for the *Liberty Gazette*, she said that "women should believe there are other missions in the world for them besides that of wife and mother." The only beliefs Adah shared with Alexander were his religious ones. She adopted his Jewish faith and remained steadfast in it until her death.

Regardless of his opinions, Alexander found himself relying on the money Adah was making when he lost his fortune in ill-advised real estate investments. Adah tried to bolster his demoralized spirit by naming him her manager, but new marital troubles were on the horizon. Adah enjoyed the adulation of her audiences and the adoration of the young men who gathered at the stage door, roses in their arms. Alexander was extremely jealous of the attention she was given. He distanced himself from his popular, independent wife when she insisted on wearing pants and on smoking in public, things proper women of the time absolutely did not do. When he could tolerate it no more, the pair separated.

Adah got over the collapse of her marriage by going on another acting tour. She traveled across the Great Plains and the West, performing in the plays *Great Expectations* and *Mazeppa*. Dressed in risqué costumes, the immodest Adah packed houses in boomtown theaters, prompting overeager critics to state, "Prudery is obsolete now." Frontier men fell in love with Adah's style, lovely face, and exquisite figure.

Adah was one of the first actresses to recognize the value of photography for both publicity and posterity. Playbills featuring her picture preceded her arrival, appearing in every newspaper and on every theater anywhere near where she was set to perform. Her portrayal of the Prince of Tartar in *Mazeppa* and a lovesick sailor boy in the play *Black-Eyed Susan* brought rave reviews from theater critics everywhere. One critic was so impressed with her daring ability to take on men's roles that he proclaimed her to be "the finest actress in the country." Victor Hippard of the *New York Sentinel Critic* wrote, "She glosses my face with laughter and tears. She is the Aphrodite the male world has waited for . . . she is a rare beauty perched upon one of Heaven's high hills of light."

When Adah wasn't acting, she was honing her writing skills, penning poems for a new book and contributing articles to a publication called *Israelite*. In these articles she called upon the Jewish people to defend themselves against injustices and prepare for the return to Zion. Her essay on Jews in Parliament that appeared in the September 3, 1858, issue was a powerful plea for the right of Jewish men to sit in the British House of Parliament as elected members. Scholars took notice of her work and often used quotes from her articles in their lectures. As pleased as she was to be taken seriously as a writer and an actress, a whirlwind affair with prizefighter John "Benicia Boy" Heenan convinced her to abandon her talents for a time to concentrate on being a wife and mother.

John was a 6-foot, 2-inch Irish man who met Adah backstage after one of her performances at the National Theater in Cincinnati. His fame as a pugilist had traveled ahead of him, and Adah was fascinated. John proposed, asking her to retire from her professions and concentrate solely on their marriage. Remarkably, she agreed and married Heenan on September 3, 1859. On their honeymoon John taught her how to box; she soon learned to hold her own and would spar with him good-humoredly. But after a month of marriage, the good humor was lost when John started beating Adah every night after dinner.

Like Alexander, John was jealous of the attention his wife received from her admiring fans. He felt threatened by the fact that his wife earned more money for her work than he did. Their stormy marriage came to an abrupt end when Alexander turned up and announced that he had never secured a divorce from Adah. The enraged boxer sailed to London to fight in the World Heavyweight Championship, leaving Adah to face the scandal alone. Alexander officially divorced Adah, and even though she was three months pregnant with John's child, Adah divorced John soon after. It was a difficult pregnancy. Adah was able to carry the baby to term and give birth to a son, but he died a few hours later.

By March 1860 Adah Menken was at the lowest point of her life and career. The *New York Sunday Mercury* published copies of her poems of despair. Critics considered her poems to be "more self-revealing than those which any other female American poet had ever dared to publish." After a long period of sorrow, Adah decided to return to the stage. She vowed to "assault the highest citadels of the theater" and to "never again be a victim or sacrifice anything for the male-dominated society." She had no idea how soon she'd be put to the test.

Adah played theaters throughout the country in lead roles in *The Soldier's Daughter* and *The French Spy*. Audiences still went wild for her. Critics called her a second Lola Montez, comparing her to the Gold Rush performer known for being bawdy and without inhibitions, and observed that "her style of acting is as free from the platitude of the stage as her poetry is from the language." Her poems and articles were distributed freely to be reprinted in the newspapers of the towns in which she performed. Her plays drew expectant crowds all across the country.

About this time Adah fell in love again, with Robert Henry Newell, the literary editor of the *New York Sunday Mercury*. After reading her poetry and watching her performances, he was convinced they were destined to be together. He thought she had the "keenest mind" he had "ever encountered in a member of her sex." Adah felt the intellectual Newell would make a fine husband, and so the two were married on September 24, 1862. During their honeymoon Newell's true intent for his wife was revealed. He insisted that she give up her career and make serving him her life's work, informing her that she could read and write only poetry in her spare time. The bride made a hasty escape.

The brief marriage was sniggered over in the press. Adah publicly acknowledged that she was not very good at choosing leading men for her own life. "Being a wife was never my most successful performance," she admitted. Her failed marriages gave her an even more liberated view of the role of women. "A man discovered America," she wrote, "but a woman equipped the voyage. So everywhere; man executes the performance, but woman trains the man. Every effectual person, leaving an impress on the world is but another Columbus, whose mind was trained and furnished by some Isabella, in the form of his Mother, Wife, or Sister. Will men never learn to be grateful?"

Adah returned to California, wanting to distance herself from bad press and the growing conflict in the East that would lead to the Civil War. Newspapers throughout Gold Country happily reported she was booked for a one-hundred-night engagement at Maguire's Opera House in San Francisco.

Tom Maguire, an important player in San Francisco's theatrical scene, was thrilled that Adah had agreed to perform at his establishment. He gave her the greatest publicity campaign ever devoted to a theatrical event in San Francisco. Before opening night the entire run was sold out. San Franciscans didn't care about her reputation; they just wanted to see her for themselves.

Although Adah's form-fitting costumes were the most risqué anyone had seen onstage since Lola Montez, Tom was not entirely satisfied and asked Adah to remove even more clothing for the benefit of the males in the audience. After a considerable increase in her salary, Adah agreed to wear only a simple blouse and a pair of shorts that revealed most of her legs. The costume was scandalous for the time and shocked the public so much that people literally fought for the privilege of seeing the "naked lady." Adah performed many roles, but no matter the part, in the last scene she'd strip down to almost nothing.

Members of an organization called the Reform Group complained that "her style belonged more to the wild old time of the Forty-Niners, than to a respectable society where many days often pass without any murders at all." Nonetheless, her unique style made her a rich woman, and she wasn't about to censor her act. Adah Menken's amazing success in California theatrical history wasn't matched until films became popular.

As her fame increased, Adah gained and lost two more husbands and had another child. She never stopped working, though, and became known as "The Frenzy of Frisco." San Francisco adopted her as its favorite daughter. The Saint Francis Hook and Ladder Company made her an honorary member of its fire-fighting brigade; she was presented with a beautiful belt, and the entire brigade, including a brass band, serenaded her.

Journalists, too, were happy with her cultivated eccentricities, and they devoted many lines of text to her. Although the Civil War was raging back East and California was pro-Union, Adah spread a large Confederate flag across one wall of her hotel room. By day she walked the streets clad only in a single yellow silk garment. "Yellow," she said, was "her mystical color," and when writer Joaquin Miller called upon her for an interview, he found her lying upon a yellow rug, clothed in a yellow sheath. He was transfixed by the costume and wrote, "I doubt if any other woman in the world could wear a dress like that in the winds of San Francisco and not look ridiculous."

Adah wasn't satisfied with being only "The Frenzy of Frisco"; she wanted to be the frenzy of the entire West. In 1864 she took to the road again, traveling east to Virginia City, Nevada. The *Gold Hill News* touted the actress's arrival on the front page: "She has come! The Menken was aboard one of the *Pioneer* coaches which reached Gold Hill this morning, at half-past eleven o'clock. She is decidedly a pretty little woman, and judging her style we supposed she does not care how she rides—she was on the front seats with her back turned to the horses. She will doubtless draw large houses in Virginia City, with her *Mazeppa* and *French Spy* in which she excels any living actresses."

Adah opened her Virginia City show on March 2, 1864. Tickets ranged in price from $1.00 for a single seat to $10.00 for a private box. The theater was packed on opening night. Many people were forced to stand in the aisles, and hundreds were turned away. Local critics, including a young Samuel Clemens (later to be known as Mark Twain), were present to review her performance. Adah was ushered onto the stage by thunderous applause. She brought down the house, and appreciative miners threw silver ingots at her feet. Sam Clemens was thoroughly impressed. His description of her performance published in the *Humboldt Register* is considered the best surviving account of Adah in action:

> I went to see her play *Mazeppa,* of course. They said she was dressed from head to foot in flesh-colored "tights," but I had no opera-glass, and I couldn't see it, to use the language of the inelegant rabble. She appeared to me to have but one garment on—a thin tight white linen one, of unimportant dimensions; I forget the name of the article, but it is indispensable to infants of tender age—I suppose any young mother can tell you what it is, if you have the moral courage to ask the question. With exception of this superfluous rag, the Menken dresses like the Greek Slave; but some of her postures are not so modest as the suggestive attitude of the latter. She is a finely formed woman down to her knees. . . .
>
> Here every tongue sings the praises of her matchless grace, her supple gestures, her charming attitudes. Well, possibly, these tongues are right. In the first act she rushes out on stage, cavorting around; she bends herself back like a bow; she pitches headforemost at the atmosphere like a battering ram; she works her arms, and her legs, and her whole body like a dancing jack; her every movement is as quick as thought. . . . If this be grace then the Menken is eminently graceful.

Adah earned an estimated $150,000 from her twenty-nine Nevada shows. When it came time for her to leave Virginia City, lovesick miners presented her with a silver brick valued at $403.31. It was stamped: MISS ADAH ISAACS MENKEN FROM FRIENDS OF VIRGINIA CITY, NEVADA TERRITORY—MARCH 30TH, 1864. Their devotion to the actress didn't end there—they named a local mine after her and formed the Menken Shaft and Tunnel Company. The company's stock certificates bore a picture of a naked lady bound to a galloping stallion. Adah left Nevada promising she'd return as soon as she could.

She traveled to Europe, still performing in *Mazeppa*, and toured Paris and Vienna. Although her talent was appreciated abroad, she never felt more loved or accepted by an audience as she had when she performed in California and Nevada.

In June 1868, while performing in her famous "nude scene," the horse Adah was bound to ran too near one of flats on the stage and the flesh of Adah's leg was torn. Later a doctor found that a cancerous growth had formed as a result of the accident. Six weeks later Adah collapsed from an advanced case of tuberculosis. She died on August 18, 1868 and was buried in Paris. She was only thirty-three years old.

Amazingly, her passing went mostly unnoticed. A brief eulogy appeared in a Paris newspaper:

> Ungrateful animals, mankind;
> Walking his rider's hearse behind,
> Mourner-in-chief her horse appears,
> But where are all her cavaliers?

Helena Modjeska

POLISH PHENOMENON

The sorcery of a genius superb in power and marvelous in grace was upon them.

—*Territorial Enterprise*, Virginia City, Nevada, October 23, 1877

A cold wind blew down the canyon, carrying pellets of frozen snow and grit from the mines in the hills surrounding Virginia City, Nevada. The wind swirled through the narrow streets, bringing damp, cold air and the smell of woodsmoke into National Guard Hall. A restless audience debated the prospects of entertainment this stormy evening. Could a Polish woman really deliver the goods tonight?

Miners with callused hands mingled with clean-fingered merchants and discussed the probabilities of a rousing performance. Gamblers watched the stage for signs that the mysterious Madame Modjeska would soon appear and wagered she would be unintelligible in the French play *Adrienne Lecouvreur*. Helena Modjeska barely spoke English, they said with knowing looks. Her English teacher had been German, they chuckled, so the odds were good that the great tragedy would become a farce.

Backstage, Helena Modjeska paced the boards, running her lines and tamping down nerves. She was more than 6,000 miles from Cracow, waiting in the wings to perform a play in front of an audience of Comstock miners about a Parisian courtesan who had died nearly fifty years before. This brawling town of Virginia City was shocking, with its gambling dens and brothels doing brisk business alongside shops, hotels, and, just one street away, churches. How could she possibly con-

HELENA MODJESKA 1840–1909

vey the pathos and the strength of the character through two language barriers in a town described as an outpost of Hell?

That she did so, and with startling success, was chronicled in the Nevada press. Barely two weeks after her thirty-seventh birthday, the *Territorial Enterprise* of October 23, 1877, presented her with a gift of unstinting praise:

> The acting of Madame Modjeska last night at National Guard Hall was not like anything ever seen before in Virginia City. It was the perfect realization of something which we fancy is dreamed of by us all, but which we have waited and waited for through the years until deep down in our hearts we have concluded it was something too rare for any earthly one to give realization to—that it was but a longing of the divine within us which only in some other state less sordid, dull and cold that this could find full expression. But last night the dream was made real, and more than once did the audience rub their eyes and look up with that questioning gaze which men put on when startled suddenly from a broken sleep.

Barely two months from her debut on the California stage, Helena Modjeska had proven she could hold an American audience in the palm of her hand as well as she had held the audiences she'd charmed in Europe. It proved, in a way, that she had made the right decision in leaving Crakow and the fame she had earned there. In only one year she had succeeded, despite launching her career for a second time in a strange land where even simple conversation with her neighbors was nearly impossible.

Helena Modjeska had conquered adversity more than once in her life. She was born October 12, 1840, and named Jadwiga Opid by her mother, Josephine Benda, who had been widowed five years before. She was the first of two daughters born several years after Josephine's husband had died, leaving their three legitimate sons fatherless. The family guardian was a schoolteacher, Michael Opid, whose name was given to Helena and her little sister. Opid had an interest in music and drama. Helena grew up with fond memories of him and his lively manner and wide-ranging interests. But she had barely hit her teens when Opid died, and the loss of property and income once again left her mother in dire financial straits.

Helena went to a convent school but yearned for a more creative life on the stage. With the blessings and help of a wealthy friend of her mother, Gustav Sinnmayer, Helena dropped out of school and began taking acting lessons.

She was eighteen years old when she and Sinnmayer left Crakow for a small town 50 miles to the east that was famed for its salt mines. At a charity fair there, she made her theatrical debut.

Then, on January 27, 1861, Helena gave birth to a son. Sinnmayer, twenty years Helena's senior, fathered the child. "He had already become as dear to me as my own brothers," she wrote in her memoirs, "and besides, my imagination adorned him with the attributes of all the impossible heroes I read about in poetry or prose."

It isn't clear whether she and Sinnmayer had married, although she implies they had in her memoirs. Sinnmayer had taken the name Modrzejewski, also Modjeski, which Helena later used in its feminine form, Modjeska, in France and America.

She later gave birth to a second child, a daughter, but her interest in a career on the stage did not wane as the demands of motherhood increased. Soon, Sinnmayer gathered a troupe of actors including some of Helena's siblings. They were very popular on tour in neighboring towns, but once again tragedy cast a pall on success.

"They say misfortunes never come singly, but are accompanied by other misfortunes, forming a long linked chain," Helena wrote. "Blow after blow struck my heart and bruised it to the core."

Helena's three-year-old daughter, Marylka, died. Sunk in grief, Helena became ill. Adding to the mental and emotional burden, her family urged her to

Helena poses in her costume for Shakespeare's As You Like It.

leave Sinnmayer. Without clearly explaining the reasons behind the separation, Helena returned to Crakow with her son Rudolph, but without Sinnmayer. With the help of relatives and friends, she was soon starring in productions at Crakow theaters. Ambitious and talented, she set her sights on the Warsaw stage.

Her passionate nature, however, led her to challenge the regime that controlled Poland. Rebelling against the political situation, Helena became popular in nationalistic plays that drew the ire of censors. Despite the danger of reprisal from tweaking the nose of authority, she continued voicing political opposition through the parts she played. Her skills and her popularity increased, but she dreamed of greater triumphs. In 1866 she left Warsaw behind, headed for Paris.

There she met a young Polish aristocrat who helped her career. Count Karol Bozenta Chlapowski, another rebel, had recently been freed from a Prussian prison, where he had been confined more than a year for engaging in revolutionary activities. Helena and Count Bozenta were kindred spirits, with strong nationalistic beliefs. They were married in 1868, and Chlapowski directed Helena's career to a pinnacle in Europe. She was earning the highest salary of any performer and was offered a life-engagement at the Imperial Theater in Warsaw.

So what was she doing in 1877 on a drafty stage in National Guard Hall in the barren hills of Nevada? Why would she leave behind assured success in the cosmopolitan cities of Europe for a risky life in the rugged mining camps of the American West?

She came to participate in the American dream of freedom and, more specifically, to live the ideal of a pastoral life in golden California. "I pictured myself a life of toil under the blue skies of California, among the hills, riding on horseback with a gun over my shoulder, I imagined all sorts of things except what was really in store for me."

The idea of peace, freedom, and happiness was a welcome change from the intense labors of the actress who was often under close watch by the secret police. During seven years in Poland, she had learned and performed 284 roles in several languages created by a variety of playwrights from Shakespeare to Goethe, as well as works from Polish dramatists. She was the center of a glittering social circle that included the leading artistic and intellectual talents of the day.

Unfortunately, her work, her social life, and worrying about the police surveillance on her husband weakened her physically and emotionally. She caught typhoid fever. Recovery was slow, but during quiet evenings at home she listened to the glowing ideas of an American utopia developed by her husband and his friend, author Henryk Sienkiewicz. In later years Sienkiewicz became a noted literary figure, most famous for writing *Quo Vadis?* but also well known for short stories based on his experiences in California.

A noble dream was conceived among the members of Helena's inner circle—that of a California farm that would house and support a colony of Polish emigrants. In her memoirs Helena says she considered the winter evening in 1875 that led to the American adventure "a stroke of fate." She half-listened while the group of friends that had gathered at her home talked, admitting she was in a "torpid state" until the conversation turned to America.

"Someone brought news of the coming Centennial Exposition in America. Sienkiewicz, with his vivid imagination, described the unknown country in the most attractive terms. Maps were brought out and California discussed. It was worthwhile to hear the young men's various opinions about the Golden West: 'You cannot die of hunger there, that is quite sure!' said one. 'Rabbits, hares and partridges are unguarded! You have only to go out and shoot them!'"

Helena's husband proposed a six-month vacation, chiefly to benefit his wife's health, but the others were intent on establishing their utopian colony. The legends of California's bounty influenced the group. Stories were told of travelers' claims about the far-off land where the "the fruit of the cactus grow wild, and they say the latter is simply delicious." The lure of a land free from war and oppression, a paradise of orange groves and abundant game, of perfect weather and untrammeled freedom coalesced into a definite plan. The die was cast, and strife-torn Poland was left behind.

In July 1876 the eight-member nucleus of the colony landed in New York and then traveled to the farm near Anaheim in southern California, where Sienkiewicz had scouted suitable property. He had gone ahead to prepare for the expatriate band's arrival at the farm he had purchased.

Unfortunately, the dream of a bountiful future failed within a year. The men of the colony were unused to working as common laborers, and their utopian dream began to crumble. By the end of the year, Helena and her husband were feeling the financial pinch. She sold her silverware to raise money and left for San Francisco in the hope of reviving her career; her aristocratic husband and their son stayed behind, living in a rustic shack in the Santa Ana hills, cooking over an open fire.

As the property was being auctioned in early 1877, Helena discovered the difficulties in gaining the attention of theater managers. Despite her proficiency in playing parts in several European languages, she didn't speak English well, and no one cared to risk a production starring a barely understandable Polish actress. It became obvious that she had to improve her ability with English, so she hired a tutor, who was German. Helena's pronunciation inevitably carried a heavy accent.

None of the San Francisco theatrical producers were impressed with a Polish "countess" they considered merely a dilettante stepping out of the society world for a brief fling with acting, especially one with an accent. Then she was introduced to Miss Josephine Tuholski, a Polish woman who spoke excellent English. "Miss Jo" tutored Helena, and their work together led to a lifelong companionship between them. A natural aptitude for languages made Helena a quick study, and in August of that same year she made her debut on the American stage in *Adrienne Lecouvreur*.

The critics were largely complimentary, although the *San Francisco Chronicle* had little regard for her acting talents:

> Few ladies have appeared on the San Francisco stage who
> have owed so much to womanly grace and sympathy and so
> little to distinguished talent.

Within a few months, however, she was on tour. Most reviews were glowing, with the occasional reservation expressed about a foreign actress. After two curtain calls at the opening of *Adrienne Lecouvreur* in Virginia City, Nevada, the *Territorial Enterprise* printed a glowing review. Another publication, however, called her acting "peculiar" and opted to observe other performances before casting a final opinion. According to the *Footlight:*

> A critic can only judge properly by comparison, and the fact that the play she appeared in was an entirely strange one prevents any extended criticism. The audience especially, are powerless to judge of her ability, unless she appear in some play in which our own great stars have appeared.

It took only one more performance to convince the *Footlight* critic, who then conceded that Helena Modjeska was a sterling artist and "indescribably womanly."

The *Reno Gazette* of October 29, 1877, quoted an unnamed "eastern dramatic writer" in the advance notice of a performance at Smith's Academy of Music in Reno:

> Her enunciation is clear and distinct, and is not impaired by naturally peculiar accentuation, and her distribution of emphasis is perfect. She has a very melodious voice with a variety of pleasing modulations. She has proved herself to be an actress of great energy, capable of fine intuitions, and long experience on the Polish stage has made her a finished artist. Her figure is lithe, supple and graceful. She has a good and very refined face, and her power of expression is remarkable.

Within six months the Polish colony near Anaheim had fragmented, but Helena's career had turned to solid gold. She went on to great acclaim in New York, where her husband joined her after finally disposing of their property. Playing

Marguerite Gauthier in the play *Camille* the way she believed the author intended, she achieved huge success, with the theater sold out weeks in advance.

The script was not universally loved by actresses who played the part, nor by audiences who were somewhat scandalized by a play about a "fallen woman." Helena wrote: "It pleased my imagination to present [Marguerite Gauthier] in *Camille* as reserved, gentle, intense in her love, and most sensitive—in one word, an exception to her kind." Her insightful performances in various roles were the result of study and a desire to strictly follow the intentions of the author of the play.

She did not like what had happened in American theater, where a "star" system had taken hold. Theater managers knew a leading actor could fill the house and exploited that fact wherever they could. Helena thought American actors never developed a good range because they followed too closely what managers dictated rather than to demand new, challenging parts in order to develop their repertoire in depth.

Otis Skinner, an actor who had worked with Helena at the Baldwin Theater in San Francisco, compared her with the leading actresses of the day who played the same parts. *Camille* was a play that had been adapted from a French novel by Alexandre Dumas, son of the man of the same name famous for *The Three Musketeers*. The French title, translated *The Lady of the Camellias*, had been shortened to *Camille* in America. It tells the story of a courtesan, Marguerite, who falls in love with a gentle young man; to be worthy of his love she tries to escape the life she has been leading. The youth's father persuades her to give him up so as not to ruin the boy's future and that of his innocent adolescent sister. Heeding the father's plea, she breaks her young lover's heart and her own by returning to her life as a courtesan and dies alone and poor, only sending him her journal at her death with the truth behind her betrayal of their love.

Modjeska dug deep to find the heart of her character, and Skinner recognized her genius:

Where Mme. Modjeska's art was greater than that of any other actress was in its womanliness, its joyousness and its limpid purity. She played Camille, even, with such serene sweetness that the unworthy in the character was forgotten and only the intrinsic womanliness of the role was presented. Mme. Sarah Bernhardt's Camille was a technical triumph. It was finished with a diamond cutter's skill, but it was theatrical, objective and studied. [Eleanora] Duse's Camille was a magnificent performance of hard, unlovely realism, which grew in effect as it grew in unpleasantness. It was big and brutal. Mme. Modjeska's Camille was the work of a poetess, whose soul, sensitive to suffering, comprehended Camille's misery and reflected it, as a pool of water reflects an object—without contamination, or offense.

Following that success, Helena's family joined her to visit Europe, but she returned several times to America, where she traveled on tour in a stylish and comfortable private railroad car. She and her husband had become naturalized citizens, and when not on tour lived again in southern California. Ironically, they had come almost full circle, for the estate they purchased in Santiago Canyon was only about 20 miles from the ill-fated utopian colony that had inspired their journey from Poland to America.

She named the new estate Arden. A large addition to the original ranch house was designed by famed architect Stanford White and included a front entrance resembling a stage, where impromptu performances took place. Helena designed gardens where she could walk in peace among her roses. She toured for twenty years, always returning to Arden to rest and recuperate from bouts of ill health. In 1888–89 she played roles she had always loved (including Lady Macbeth, Ophelia, Beatrice, Viola, Portia, and Rosalind) while on tour with Edwin Booth, the great Shakespearean actor.

Her great skill in holding an audience came from her deep belief in playing a part in such a natural way that the audience tended to forget they were watching a drama. Each role was analyzed and rehearsed to spellbinding perfection. Once, she recalled after the birth of her son's first child, she had half-jokingly promised that she would convincingly play Juliet when she had become a grandmother. She succeeded because her ability transcended the knowledge of the audience that she was not the teenager in love that Shakespeare had so accurately portrayed with his pen.

The *Territorial Enterprise* of Nevada recognized that ability during her first appearances in America in 1877. Following the performances in windswept Virginia City, the jokes about a Polish-born actress died away. Said the *Enterprise* critic:

> The audience listened as to an incantation and went away believers in enchantment. We cannot, in a brief and hurried notice, give any idea of the acting of Madame Modjeska. She is a lady of wonderful mind, and that mind has been trained in the severe discipline of the European schools, until art has become so perfect that it seems like nature.

The freedoms of America were as important to Helena and her husband as the money earned on the stage. Still, despite her long and successful career in America, a large corner of her heart belonged to Poland. As it had been when she and her husband had been shadowed by secret police for their outspoken views on the heavy-handed Prussian regime, her voice was raised again at the World's Columbian Exposition at Chicago in 1893. She drew a large crowd impatient to see the woman who had reportedly mesmerized an audience simply by reciting the Polish alphabet. Her unusual speech galvanized the audience even though it delved into international affairs and foreign policy. She censured those who oppressed her native land and its women.

In 1907 she and her husband left their Santiago Canyon retreat and moved to a small home on Bay Island, near Newport Beach. Although her health had improved during the years in America, she was ill much of the time and saw few visitors. Helena Modjeska died on April 9, 1909, and her remains were returned to Poland, where they were interred in Crakow, the city of her birth.

Lucille Mulhall

COWGIRL

Little Miss Mulhall, who weighs only ninety pounds, can break a bronc, lasso and brand a steer and shoot a coyote at 500 yards. She can also play Chopin, quote Browning, and make mayonnaise.

—*New York World*, July 7, 1900

A pair of large, mean steers burst out of the gate and raced onto the parade field. Eighteen-year-old Lucille Mulhall bolted after the beasts atop her trained horse, Governor. The beautiful blond with petite features and blue-gray eyes quickly tossed the lasso she was twirling and snagged one of the animals around its neck. The steer jerked to a stop as Governor planted his feet firmly on the ground. Lucille leapt at the steer with another rope and began to tie its feet together. In thirty seconds she had completed the task, breaking the steer-roping record at the rodeo grounds in Denison, Texas.

On a hot September day in 1903, Lucille won the Grayson County Fair's roping contest, beating out two of the top cowboys in the county in the process. She was awarded a pendant of gold with a raised star in which was imbedded a diamond. In the center of the pendant was a steer-roping scene set in blue enamel. It was a prize she wore with pride for the rest of her career.

Lucille Mulhall was destined to be a cowgirl. Her father, Zack Mulhall, had her on the back of a horse before she could walk. She was born on October 21,

LUCILLE MULHALL   1885–1940

1885, and raised on her family's 80,000-acre ranch near Guthrie, Oklahoma. At an early age she showed a talent for horse riding. She was a natural in the saddle, at training horses, roping, branding cattle, and all the other chores associated with ranch hands. History records that she was extremely bright and could have gone on to be a teacher, but she preferred cowboying, and with her father's help, she made it her life's work.

After a successful roping-and-riding contest in 1899, Zack decided this form of entertainment had massive monetary potential. He put together a group of horseback performers and called them Mulhall's Congress of Rough Riders and Ropers. Lucille was a part of this group and began her career at a riding exhibition in Oklahoma City. She was fourteen years old.

A few months after Zack's rodeo took to the road, he added a variety of other acts to the Rough Riders show, including a cowboy band and comedians, storytellers, and trick ropers. Will Rogers was among the storytellers and trick ropers initially hired. Will and Lucille became fast friends, and he was quite taken with her horseback-riding ability. "Lucille was just a kid when we began working together," he wrote. "She was riding her pony all over the place . . . it was the direct start of what has since come to be known as the Cowgirl."

On July 4, 1900, Lucille's career got an unexpected boost from a high-profile political leader. Vice-presidential candidate Theodore Roosevelt was in Oklahoma City for a reunion of his Rough Riders cavalry regiment from the Spanish American War and attended a rodeo in which Zack Mulhall's horsemen and women were the key entertainment. When Lucille rode into the arena, she instantly stole the show, and Roosevelt's admiration. He was so impressed with her skill that he urged Zack to travel across America with his child so that everyone could see the "wonderful girl." It was advice Zack was quick to take.

With Lucille as the star, Mulhall's Congress of Rough Riders and Ropers was a highly sought-after rodeo. The group toured extensively through Colorado, Washington, and Texas. Lucille and her horse captivated audiences with their speed and precision. In less than a year, she was the best-known cowgirl performer in the West.

Lucille worked with Governor day and night, teaching him new tricks all the time. He was a highly intelligent, chestnut-brown animal with a white forehead and white feet. He had more than forty tricks in his repertoire. He could pull off a man's coat and put it back on the person again, walk up and down stairs, and sit with his forelegs crossed. Fascinated reporters attempted to describe the phenomenon that was Lucille's act in their newspapers, but they weren't sure what to call her. "The Female Conqueror of Beef and Horn," "Cowboy Girl," and "The Ranch Queen" were some of the phrases they came up with. After she won three gold medals for steer-roping, a trophy for cutting horses, and a belt buckle declaring her to be the "best female horsewoman" to date, Zack began to bill his daughter as "The Champion Lady Rider and Roper of the World." Posters announcing the Mulhall rodeo's arrival prominently featured her new title.

The exhibitions Lucille performed in were dangerous. In addition to roping and riding, she participated in mock stagecoach robberies in which she played an outlaw who ended up being shot off her horse. When asked by newspaper reporters if she was ever afraid her horse would slip out and fall, she replied, "I expect that, I'm not afraid of getting hurt."

In 1902 Lucille had an accident that would have caused any professional rider to give up the sport. It happened during a relay race in St. Louis when she was dismounting a bronco. On October 20 the *St. Louis Star* reported what happened:

> Fully 15,000 spectators saw the pretty form of the plucky young girl roll in the dust of the mile track. It is thought that Miss Mulhall was struck by the pony of one of the cowboys, and the muscles and tendons of her ankle were torn away and the limb badly bruised.
>
> The relay race had two entries besides Miss Mulhall. At each quarter mile the riders took fresh mounts. Miss Mulhall was in the middle, and as she jumped from her

pony, one of the cowboys thundered by, unable to swerve his
pony. The girl's slight body was under the horse's feet. She
was taken to her home in her father's buggy. Plucky to the
last, she insisted on driving the rig herself.

Lucille was absent from several rodeo performances after the accident, but she
could always be found watching from the stands with her leg in a cast.

At the age of seventeen, Lucille was a four-year veteran of a Wild West show.
Theodore Roosevelt remembered the "petite rider" and asked her to perform at his
inauguration ceremony when he was elected president of the United States. Her
popularity grew considerably after the presidential performance, and fans hoarded
photographs of her that appeared in magazines and newspapers.

Lucille was constantly adding new routines to her act. She learned to pick up
money, pins, and other objects off the ground while riding full speed on horseback.
The highlight of her program was a roping contest between herself and four men.
The program concluded with a skit about the hanging of a horse thief. Lucille
would lasso the thief and drag him from his horse. Crowds always jumped to their
feet with excitement during the skit.

Although Lucille preferred the rough and dangerous life of the rodeo, she was
feminine and soft-spoken. Several newspaper articles made mention of her style and
fine manners. The *El Paso Daily* wrote of her "big, blue-gray eyes that look straight
at you, a tanned smooth skin that shows the marks of the sun in small freckles; a
small mouth and teeth that are as white as a wolf's; a determined chin, and a forehead in which perception and reflection are both well marked. She is slightly above
average height and weights 130 pounds. Her figure is symmetrical and her every
movement lady-like and graceful. She walks as lightly and easily as she rides."

Lucille had many suitors, but her allegiance was to her father and the rodeo
show first. She didn't enter into a serious relationship until she was twenty-two, and
even then she kept the romance a secret from her family. Zack often ran interference
between his daughter and the young men interested in courting her. He was protec-

Cowgirl Lucille worked with her horse, Governor, day and night, teaching him more than forty tricks, including walking up and down stairs and sitting with his forelegs crossed.

tive of Lucille and didn't want her settling down too soon.

Her busy schedule kept her mind off matters of the heart. She performed at such prestigious venues as Madison Square Garden, the World's Fair in St. Louis, and in Washington, D.C. Among the celebrated people she rode with were movie star Tom Mix and Apache Indian Chief Geronimo.

In 1906 Mulhall's Congress of Rough Riders and Ropers disbanded. The show had become tiresome for many of its participants, and they decided to go in different directions. Lucille returned to the family ranch for awhile, but she was soon lured back into show business by her father when an offer came for her to join a vaudeville review. The announcement of her return to the spotlight appeared in newspapers across the country. The *Wichita Eagle* wrote:

> Miss Lucille Mulhall's engagements will begin on January 20 in the Orpheum at Kansas City, where her father has completed a contract for her appearance in a number of cities. The vaudeville act will be modeled after the wild west show in which she has taken part so often.

Lucille's new show was billed as "Lucille Mulhall and Her Ranch Boys." In addition to Lucille the troupe consisted of her two sisters, her brother, and a cowboy baritone named Martin Van Bergen. Several horses and props were a part of the entourage, as well. Theaters had to be adapted to accommodate the show. A unique portable fence designed to hang from the fly loft and fasten between the stage and orchestra pit was installed at each venue. Several inches of dirt had to be spread out over the stage floor.

Martin Van Bergen opened the show by riding out on a white horse and singing "My Lucille." During the song a spotlight followed Lucille as she rode slowly across the back of the stage. At the end of the song, Martin would hurry off, and Lucille and Governor would then perform a variety of stunts.

Lucille and Martin were smitten with each other from the start. He was impressed with Lucille's beauty and talent as a horsewoman. She fell in love with his appealing sweetness and captivating singing voice. The two were secretly married on September 14, 1907. Fearing her father would not approve, the couple kept their marriage a secret for a time, but persistent questions by the press made it impossible to conceal the union for longer than six months.

On January 29, 1909, their son, William Logan Van Bergen, was born. Lucille did not enjoy being a wife and mother. She planned to return to the rodeo program in the spring. She did, leaving her son in the care of his father and her in-laws. Her show played every major city across the United States, and she spent so much time away from home that it began to take a toll on her marriage. Then her professional career began to falter, as well.

During a matinee show in Chicago, Lucille accidentally killed a steer in the arena, prompting the Society for Prevention of Cruelty to Animals to press charges against her. A Chicago newspaper reported:

> Several hundred men, women and children saw a badly frightened steer killed yesterday at the Coliseum by the woman roper, Lucille Mulhall. When the animal, struggling feebly as it was dragged about the ring by the young woman, gave a convulsive gasp and became unconscious, a cry of disgust and horror arose from the audience, and a dozen cowboys rushed forward and dragged the carcass from the arena.

A judge immediately dismissed the charges against Lucille, but public opinion was quick to turn against her. The incident wounded her reputation and prompted a state law against steer-roping in Illinois.

Hoping to distance herself from the bad publicity, Lucille abandoned her program and joined a troupe called California Frank's All Star Wild West Show. By 1911 she no longer spent any time with her husband or son. William grew up knowing little about her. Martin held out hope that Lucille's devotion would shift from the rodeo life to domestic life, but it never happened. He filed for divorce on March 28, 1914.

Between theater engagements that same month, Lucille entered a roping contest in Walla Walla, Washington. She was twenty-eight years old and still quick with a lariat. Her best steer-roping time was thirty-three seconds. Her popularity was quick to return, though it slowed down again when World War I sidetracked the nation. Still, she performed in rodeos and showed no sign of wanting to give up her profession even if audience numbers weren't as high as they once had been.

In 1919 she married a prominent cattle and oil man named Thomas L. Burnett. She proved to be no better a wife the second time around, choosing again to travel with a rodeo she was now managing. Burnett divorced her three years later.

From 1920 to 1930 Lucille continued to perform in both her own vaudeville productions and with established troupes like the 101 Ranch Real Wild West Show and the Passing of the West program.

In 1932 Lucille suffered several devastating blows. Her beloved parents died within less than a year of each other, and the Great Depression depleted the resources of the family ranch. Brokenhearted and in poor health, Lucille found herself living in poverty, and she turned to alcohol for solace. By the spring of 1935, she had pulled herself together and accepted an offer from her hometown of Guthrie, Oklahoma, to lead its annual Frontier Celebration Day parade. An excerpt from local newspaper reporter Noel Houston's column described the aging cowgirl's return to the saddle:

> Once she was a vivacious, devil may-care blonde in a divided
> skirt and white silk shirt as she passed in review before
> kings, presidents and worshipping throngs. The thoughtless
> observer might see her now as only a gray, time-penciled old
> woman. But as she rode at the head of the frontier celebra-
> tion in her traditional costume—beaded jacket over a white
> silk waist, red corduroy skirt draping below her boot tops—
> Miss Mulhall was beautiful to me.

Encouraged by the crowd's response to her parade appearance, Lucille agreed to join her brother's Wild West show. Now fifty years old, she participated only in special acts and didn't take part in the rodeos as a contestant. With her life and career back on track, she worked steadily, entertaining audiences and training horses. After more than forty years in the saddle, she was one of the most revered and fearless horsewomen in the world.

On December 21, 1940, Lucille was on her way back to the family ranch when a truck broadsided the car she was riding in, killing her instantly. On a cold, rainy day, she was laid to rest alongside her parents. Few attended her graveside funeral, but a notice in the *Daily Oklahoman* newspaper described the sad, somewhat ironic scene:

> A machine killed Lucille Mulhall, but horses brought her to her final resting place. So deep was the mud and so slippery the road, that a neighbor's plow horse had to pull the hearse from the highway to near the house, and the car bearing the relatives had to be pulled back to the highway after the services.

Lucille received the greatest honor of her career in 1975, when she was inducted into the National Cowboy Hall of Fame. Her accomplishments are still greatly admired by rodeo enthusiasts.

Kate Rockwell

FLAME OF THE YUKON

Centered in the spotlight, draped in a long, rose-colored evening gown with a magnificent ostrich-plumed hat outlining her oval face, Kate endeared herself to the sourdoughs by crooning songs of far away places in her low, sultry voice. The miners stamped their feet, cheered and threw quantities of gold nuggets at her feet.

—*Alaska Today*, 1901

A frigid wind blew hard past the weather-beaten exterior of the Palace Garden Theater in Dawson City, Alaska. It was the spring of 1900, and gleeful patrons were tucked warmly inside, waiting for the "Flame of the Yukon" to take the stage.

A feisty, red-headed beauty glided out before the crowd, her violet eyes smiling. The men went wild with applause. The music began, and the entertainer swayed with the beat, placing a gloved hand to her breast and a fingertip to her lips and then, stretching her arm out, beckoning her admirers. The elaborate red-sequin dress she was wearing was form-fitting, and the long black cape that draped over her shoulders clung to her alabaster skin.

The piano player accelerated his playing, and Kate gyrated gracefully in and out of the shadows of the colored lights that flicked across the stage. After a moment, with a slight movement of her hand, she dropped the cape off her shoulders and it fell to the floor. The glittering diamonds and rhinestones around her

KATE ROCKWELL 1876–1957

neck sparkled and shined. Ever so seductively she picked up a nearby cane adorned with more than 200 yards of red chiffon and began leaping, while twirling the fabric-covered walking stick. Around and around she fluttered, the chiffon trailing wildly about her like flames from a fire, the material finally settling over her outstretched body. The audience erupted in a thunderous ovation. She was showered with nuggets and pouches filled with gold dust. This dance would make her famous.

Kathleen Eloisa Rockwell came to the Klondike in April 1900. She attracted a following wherever she performed across Alaska. Kate was born in Junction City, Kansas, on October 4, 1876, to parents of Scottish-Irish descent. Her love for music and dancing began when she was a toddler. The piano and scratchy gramophone had an intoxicating effect on her. Her wealthy stepfather provided the gifted child with the education she needed to hone her natural talents. She was trained in French and voice and instrumental music at the Osage Mission in Kansas.

Kate's parents eventually moved to Spokane, Washington, leaving their daughter behind to complete her studies. She visited her family during the summer months, when Spokane was abuzz with entertainment opportunities. Inspired by performances by traveling troupes of vaudevillians who sang and danced their way across the Northwest, she dreamed about joining the troubadours and of someday being a New York stage actress. Her dreams, however, were temporarily dashed. A stock market crash in the late 1800s left her stepfather destitute and unable to continue paying for her musical education, so she had to drop out of school.

Much to her mother's chagrin, the setback did not dampen Kate's desire to go to New York. Kate told her mother she believed she'd been born to make other people happy. Martha, Kate's mother, however, considered the theater to be a wicked place, inhabited by riffraff and immoral women. When Kate left Washington for the East Coast, Martha insisted on accompanying her as a chaperone.

Once the pair was settled in New York, Martha found work in a shirt factory and Kate answered an advertisement for a chorus girl at a nearby theater. Her natural ability, good figure, and warm personality landed her the job, which paid $18 a week.

Kate enjoyed her time on the stage and quickly became addicted to the nightlife of the big city. Martha's controlling nature kept the free-spirited Kate from having as much fun as the other cast members, and after a time it strained the mother-daughter relationship. Kate's troupe decided to take their act on the road, and they wanted Kate to come with them. She escaped her mother's watchful eye and joined her fellow entertainers in Philadelphia, changing her name to Kitty Phillips so that she couldn't be found.

Kate traveled across the Great Plains states, working her way back and forth across the country. She stood out among the other singers and dancers by always holding her head up high and smiling proudly for the appreciative audiences. Frank Calvert, one of Kate's biographers, wrote of the effect she had on theatergoers. "Without your knowledge," he explained, "she captured your heart so that shortly you were loving her and utterly taken in by her charm."

While at Coney Island, Kate received word from a girlfriend that dancers were needed at a theater in Spokane. Restless and bored with the show she was in, Kate decided to return to Washington.

At Kate's request the theater manager sent her a contract and advance pay to cover her travel expenses. Kate was amazed by what she found when she arrived. The "theater" was a minuscule stage in the back of a saloon. She would be required to work the bar between acts for a percentage of the profits from the beer she sold. She threatened to leave right away, but the manager reminded her of the signed contract in his pocket. Kate had no choice but to stay on.

Her pleasing personality and beautiful face helped sell a lot of beer. Soon Kate was rolling in money. Enticed by further financial gain, she ended up staying longer than she'd planned. She sent for her mother and changed her last name back to Rockwell. Once the contract was up, Kate traveled to Seattle to perform at the People's Theater there.

Not long after she arrived in Seattle, the Savoy Theater in British Columbia invited her to join their vaudeville troupe. She was promised great pay and the opportunity to introduce two new song-and-dance routines each week. This was the break she'd been waiting for. She signed with the company, leaving the People's Theater after only two weeks.

Then Kate came down with a serious case of gold fever. A gold rush had hit Alaska Territory, and Kate was eager to get in on the quest for riches. There was a demand for entertainers in the mining towns across the Yukon, and Kate believed she could earn a fortune filling that need. She sailed for Skagway, Alaska, aboard a crowded supply vessel with her singing and dancing partner, Gertie Jackson. The two had developed an act they were sure would attract large audiences.

The women found the conditions in Skagway less than hospitable. The streets were unpaved, buildings that housed businesses were little more than shacks, and crime was rampant. Gertie abandoned the act shortly after the duo found work. She hated Skagway and headed back for "civilization" aboard the next steamer.

Kate stayed in Alaska, determined to make her way across the territory to the mining camps where the richest gold strikes were being made. She earned money to continue her journey by working at saloons and makeshift theaters, perfecting her "buck and wing" (tap) dancing. She did an average of twenty shows a day and after a year and a half raised more than $20,000—enough money to fund her own string of theaters. Miners in Whitehorse, Alaska, were so captivated by her singing, dancing, and kindness to the down and out that they memorialized her by writing her name with champagne corks on the ceiling of a hotel in town.

In the spring of 1900, the Savoy Theater again invited Kate to join them. The company was passing through Whitehorse on their way to a playhouse in Dawson and felt she would be the perfect addition to their show. The Savoy was the largest burlesque and musical troupe ever to invade the Klondike. It was made up predominantly of pretty girls who danced, sang, acted, juggled, and did magic tricks. The troupe was welcomed with great fanfare when they arrived in Dawson. The formerly empty theater was quickly transformed into the liveliest spot in town.

Kate won over the rowdy audiences, filled with merchants, gamblers, and sour-

Kate Rockwell achieved notoriety with her "Flame Dance," in which she draped herself with red chiffon, twirled a fabric-covered walking stick, and jumped and fluttered around the stage.

doughs, with her tearful ballads and quick-stepping dance moves, sealing her fame as "Klondike Kate." (Kate Rockwell was just one of around seventeen women who went by the name "Klondike Kate" in the early 1900s. Some historians insist the real "Klondike Kate" was Katy Ryan, a girl who went to the Yukon looking for adventure in 1898 and became renowned for her selfless acts of courage trying to save sick miners from death.) There Kate introduced her famous Flame Dance. Night after night men poured in from the goldfields to watch the tempestuous singer-dancer whirl about the stage. She was the most popular act of the Savoy show and earned $200 a week. She was such a sensation that the Dawson theater manager paid tribute to her on the placard in front of the playhouse: KLONDIKE KATE IS A BIT OF THISTLE DOWN BLOWN ON A SUMMER ZEPHYR. A POEM OF LOVELINESS, AND ELYSIAN SYMPHONY OF MATCHLESS CONTOUR AND BEWITCHING BEAUTY—DIMPLED SHOULDERS AND SNOW-WHITE ARMS.

Kate Rockwell had many suitors, but her heart settled on a waiter named Alexander Pantages, who worked at the theater. Alexander was a handsome Greek man with thick, black hair. He was attentive to and protective of Kate, and she was captivated by his good looks and charming accent. He had come to Alaska seeking a fortune in gold. Unable to find it using a pick and shovel, he found other enterprising ways to hit the mother lode. When a miner asked to buy the current copy of a Seattle newspaper from him for $10, Alexander saw his chance to make money. He packed a dance hall with news-hungry miners and charged them $2.00 apiece to listen to him read the paper. He also worked at the Savoy.

Alexander dreamed of owning a chain of playhouses—a dream he had in common with Kate. She was the undisputed queen of the dance-hall girls and capable of making big money. He made plans to capitalize on her talents and affection for him.

The couple moved in together when Alexander was fired from the Savoy for skimping on the drinks. He promised to marry Kate as soon as he found other employment. In the meantime Kate supported her man in high fashion. Her act became even more popular, especially when she added a fast-paced roller-skating routine. She never failed to fill the Savoy with people and enchant her audience with throaty songs sung in tearful seriousness. Kate was earning more money than any other entertainer in Alaska.

She and Alexander opened a theater of their own, calling the place the Orpheum. Kate produced and directed her own stage show, and the Orpheum quickly became the hottest spot in Dawson. Kate sang and danced to numbers such as "There'll Be a Hot Time in the Old Town Tonight" and "Put Your Arms around Me, Honey." Within a couple of months, Alexander as manager and Kate as entertainer were bringing in $8,000 per week.

Alexander and Kate were a professional success, but their personal relationship began to falter. He had postponed their marriage several times, and Kate was growing impatient. He told Kate that he wanted to put off their wedding until they had acquired more theaters and attained a more comfortable lifestyle.

The pair took Kate's variety act to Nome (where more gold was being found) and then to San Francisco. They bought theaters in each location and then traveled across the United States, scouting out potential playhouse locations. They registered at various hotels as husband and wife. Finally, they decided to settle in Seattle. Alexander returned to Dawson to take care of their business affairs while Kate traveled to Washington alone.

While passing through Vancouver, British Columbia, Kate purchased a quaint nickelodeon that included a Biograph machine for showing moving pictures. This new form of entertainment, along with her own vaudevillian act, appealed to patrons, and in no time the theater was turning a profit. At first Alexander was furious at Kate for buying the nickelodeon; he thought the Biograph was a passing oddity. He changed his mind, however, when he saw how much money the business was making. He bought a second movie house in Seattle called the Crystal Theater, beginning the largest, most memorable chain in American entertainment history.

In the fall of 1903, Alexander booked his star, Klondike Kate, at a theater in Texas, where black gold was producing a boom. He needed her to earn more money for his theater ventures. Still hoping that he would marry her, Kate was happy to oblige. In Texas she introduced a new dance called the Butterfly Dance, during which layers of chiffon wrapped around her pink-satin gown made her appear to hover over the stage as she spun to an orchestral accompaniment. The soft, light material looked like wings as she gracefully waved her arms.

Alexander knew how to give the public what it wanted. He'd known Kate's Butterfly Dance would be popular in the booming oil towns. He hoped they would also welcome a seventeen-year-old violinist named Lois Mendenhall he had discovered. He arranged for the lovely musician to share the variety show stage in Galveston with Kate.

Kate took the dark-eyed beauty under her wing, helping her with her act and looking out for her well-being. Little did Kate know the impact this young woman would have on her life.

After more than a year of performing in Texas, Kate returned to Seattle. Alexander had put the money she'd sent home to good use, expanding their business holdings to include theaters in Portland, Tacoma, and Spokane. While Kate was performing at a Spokane theater, she received the heartbreaking news that Alexander had married someone else—none other than young Lois Mendenhall.

Kate was devastated and temporarily gave up the stage. She sank into a deep depression, growing weak from lack of nourishment and sleep. She stopped caring about her appearance and started drinking heavily. One of Kate's friends from her chorus-girl days helped snap her out of her despair long enough to take Alexander to court.

On May 26, 1905, a little more than two months after the marriage, Kate filed a $25,000 breach-of-promise lawsuit against Alexander. Alexander denied that he'd ever known her. Kate's fans were outraged. A front page article in the *Seattle Times* carried the headline: "Uses Her Money, Then Jilts the Girl."

Kate was nicknamed "Klondike Kate" during her stage tour of Alaska's gold rush country.

Once all the testimony was heard, the court dismissed the case against Alexander and rejected any financial claim Kate had. The judge ruled that there wasn't enough physical evidence to prove Alexander had consented to marry Kate or that he had used her money in his business. Kate left the courtroom a shattered and demoralized woman. She would never be the same again.

Almost a year after Kate was jilted, she returned to the stage, teaming up with comedian Arthur Searles. They performed skits and song-and-dance routines on the vaudeville circuit. Unfortunately, audiences were more interested in silent movies by this time. Kate was eventually forced to retire from show business, trading in the spotlight for a small farm in Bend, Oregon. She married twice; one union ended with her husband's death, and the other ended in divorce. She kept busy tending to her homestead, and she periodically traveled to Dawson and Seattle to visit family and friends.

While her entertainment career had stalled, Alexander's was reaching its peak. His chain of show-houses had spread all over the West. "Going to the Pantages" (Alexander's last name) was a common expression for going to the theater. Kate grew heartsick every time she heard it.

Just when Kate believed the world had forgotten about her, she received an invitation to a celebration being held in her honor in Portland. It was 1931, some thirty years after the "Flame of the Yukon" had burst onto the scene. More than a thousand fans and supporters convened in the banquet hall of the Multnomah Hotel to pay tribute to the entertainer who had lifted the spirits of the Alaska miners.

A speaker at the event introduced Kate:

> Comrades . . . up there we shared with our neighbor our cabins, our grub, and our money. But when we returned south most of us conformed. Her Klondike gold has vanished, but the sourdough spirit of her youth lives on unchanged. To us

she was laughter and beauty and song. She was forgetfulness
of hardship and homesickness. . . . Comrades, it is my honor
and pleasure to present her again tonight. Klondike Kate, the
sweetheart of the sourdoughs.

Kate was moved to tears by the kind words as she took the stage. The audience gave her a standing ovation and serenaded her with a chorus of "Let Me Call
You Sweetheart." Her spirits lifted, Kate returned briefly to the theater. She traveled
the West as a speaker, telling stories from her life and signing old photographs of
herself. In 1943 her life story was told in a film aptly titled *Klondike Kate*.

On February 21, 1957, Kate Rockwell died peacefully in her sleep. She was
eighty years old. Prominent magazines like *Time* and *Newsweek* ran articles about her
passing. *The Bulletin* newspaper in Bend, Oregon, conceded that she would never be
forgotten and predicted that her story would grow as memories of the Alaska Gold
Rush faded into distant history.

Lillian Russell

AMERICA'S BEAUTY

If a woman gets the reputation of being a professional beauty, it is hard work to live up to it.

—Lillian Russell, *The Theatre Magazine*, 1905

The green silk robe shimmered in the light of the dressing room. Adjusting the neckline, Lillian Russell glanced into the mirror and considered the interviewer's question about beauties never appreciating their good looks. "I think they do," she countered. "They are glad to have it, as they are grateful for any other gift. I am pleased and gratified when someone says I look nice."

Looking "nice" was a part of the job that the corn-fed beauty from America's heartland never forgot. The costume she wore in the second act of *Lady Teazle* showed off her abundant charms to perfection. But the green silk, the large, plumed hat, and the ebony walking stick adorned with orange ribbons were but a pretty frame for the statuesque blond performer whose sumptuous exterior diverted attention from a sharp mind and a warm heart.

As she continued dressing for the second act of the play, she answered questions from Miss Ada Patterson, longtime reporter for *The Theatre Magazine*. How, asked Patterson, had a girl from Iowa earned the name "America's Beauty"?

"I came away from Clinton when I was six months old, and I don't remember much about it," she told the reporter. A backward glance over a smooth white shoulder gave a glimpse of the famous smile, curving perfect lips. A spark of mischief

LILLIAN RUSSELL   1861–1922

flashed in the beautiful blue eyes framed by long, thick eyelashes as she added, "Although there are Tabbies who say they remember my life there when I was six months old sixty years ago."

The feature later published in *The Theatre Magazine* of February 1905 never came right out and said that America's most famous beauty was now forty-three years old. Behind her lay phenomenal success as well as heartbreak and failure, yet none of it dimmed the glow. The interviewer that day compared the throat and shoulders rising from the green silk to the *Venus de Milo*. The pure soprano voice still hit high C with ease. And, after more than twenty-three years on stage, the name Lillian Russell still drew people to the theater.

Lillian Russell's thoughts on beauty were avidly read by women all over America when Ada Patterson's interview appeared. The reporter described how the girl christened Helen Louise Leonard demonstrated the proper placement of an enormous hat atop a cluster of golden curls. Adjusting the tilted brim, the star gently lectured the reporter about her theories on good looks. "But what is beauty? It is nothing compared to intelligence and a manner. Meet a woman who has intelligence and a beautiful manner, and who stops to think whether she is beautiful or not?"

One set of admirers could testify to the gracious manner, warm heart, and generosity of the star named Lillian Russell. She was notoriously kind to people who worked for her, even when they stole from her, as one did. Yet, another group that she did business with, theater producers and promoters, knew they were dealing with a hard-driving woman who understood exactly what she was worth and made them pay her price. It was her voice, her looks, and her reputation that could ask for, and receive, huge sums for appearances on stage even when beautiful, talented, younger women contested her reign.

Helen Louise Leonard had the kind of beauty that stopped traffic from her earliest years. And she had a voice that her mother, Cynthia Rowland Leonard, an ardent feminist, paid to have trained when her fifth daughter was still in her teens. Helen Louise was educated at the Convent of the Sacred Heart in Chicago and attended finishing school at Park Institute. She took singing lessons and sang in the church choir at the Episcopal Church. She was the apple of her father Charlie's eye, his "airy, fairy Nellie," the youngest daughter with the looks and the voice of an angel.

Her parents separated when she was in her teens, and her mother took Helen Louise and moved to New York, where young Helen started training for grand opera. She could sustain the highest notes with virtually no effort, and do it again and again without strain. Her voice coach, Dr. Leopold Damrosch, told her mother that with a few years of training, he could make her a diva to rival the best.

But the beautiful blond from Iowa had other ideas. Years of training and rehearsals, with only bit parts and backup roles as an understudy lay before her on the road to stardom in opera. Helen Louise ignored her mother's plans and made her own career choice by secretly joining the Park Theater Company in Brooklyn. She was eighteen when she danced onstage for the first time in the chorus of *H.M.S Pinafore*, a Gilbert and Sullivan operetta that went on to resounding success. A neighbor of Cynthia Leonard told her about a young woman who resembled her daughter appearing in the new play he'd seen. The secret came out when her mother, fuming, rose from a seat in the audience and shouted out, "That's my Nell!"

Cynthia and her daughter were often at odds. "Mothers are good for an actress to have near until they are sixteen," Lillian later said, "and after that they are apt to be a nuisance."

Her feminist mother thought a career in light opera was beneath her daughter, but the principles of independence she'd taught had obviously found fertile ground. Eager to dive into this new life that had opened before her, not only did Helen Louise continue onstage, she took a fateful step that nearly sundered her relationship with her mother. She accepted a proposal of marriage shortly before the end of *Pinafore*'s run in 1879.

Although a handsome millionaire was courting her, she married the company's musical director, Harry Braham. That marked the end of her appearance in the chorus. She withdrew from the company and settled into domestic life, a life she was born for, according to her friend, actress Marie Dressler.

Soon Helen Louise was pregnant, and a baby son was born. Despite Dressler's opinion about Helen's natural domestic tendencies, a nurse was hired to care for the baby so that the actress could once again take up her career. Her paycheck made a big difference for the little family. Her much older husband was not happy with that decision, but a woman raised to be independent was not easily swayed when fame and fortune called.

Then one day she returned to find her baby desperately ill. Despite all attempts to cure the infant, he died in convulsions. Apparently the inexperienced nurse had accidentally pierced his abdomen with a diaper pin. Harry Braham accused his wife of neglect.

Grieving over the death of her son, feeling betrayed by her husband's accusations, beset by her mother's vitriolic accusations against Braham, Helen concentrated on her career. Tony Pastor, legendary producer of musical comedy, heard her sing at the home of a friend and consequently offered her a job. Her mother argued for a return to the career path she'd planned for her daughter in grand opera, but Helen Louise liked the immediate success she'd already tasted in comic opera. At nineteen, with a statuesque figure, golden curls, skin like "roses and cream," and a soprano voice that could do everything with ease, she had found her first mentor in Tony Pastor.

Pastor's theater specialized in send-ups of popular plays like *The Pirates of Penzance,* produced by Pastor as *The Pie Rats of Penn-Yann.* The impresario thought Helen Louise Leonard too dowdy and provincial a name for the gorgeous blond with the voice of an angel. In 1880 Pastor presented her as "Lillian Russell, the English Ballad Singer." She chose the two names from a list, later saying she liked the way the name began and ended with the same letter. Pastor gave her parts that showed off her talents. She was a rousing success, so much so that Pastor feared she would be spoiled by adulation. Instead of continuing to build her reputation in New York, he sent her west with Willie Edouin's touring company. As she traveled

Lillian Russell was known for her stunning natural beauty, but those who knew her said she was intelligent and worldly, as well. She ran for mayor of New York in 1915.

by rail toward the Pacific Ocean, she learned to play poker and pinochle.

In San Francisco Lillian Russell became the toast of the town. The City by the Bay was bubbling over with brash enterprise, fueled by newly made fortunes dug from the golden hills. The troupe that played *Babes in the Woods* and *Fun in a Photograph Gallery* earned recognition in the newspapers, and reporters took note of the fresh, young singer who made several appearances:

> There is a pretty young girl, a Miss Lillian Russell, who has a voice as sweet and fresh as a thrush, but Miss Russell sings everything too fast and loses half the effect she might give.

The same review in *The Argonaut* took note of her costumes, reporting that they were

> very pretty, pale blue satin painted with poppies and hat to match, a paler blue satin with trailing vines and morning glories, and another hat to match, and a pretty affair of pink and white and swansdown.

Unfortunately, financial disaster stalked Willie Edouin's troupe, which even the newspapers noted. Said one supporter:

> Willie Edouin has been struggling manfully against small business at the Standard. He has one of the cleverest companies I have seen here.

The report took note of Edouin's newest performer:

> And pretty Miss Lillian Russell, who is Mrs. Braham in private, has a mezzo soprano voice of beautiful quality and immense promise.

The promise of financial reward did not pay out. The *San Francisco Call* noted:

The performances of this company have been, in many instances, exceptionally clever, and, only, because of the presence in our city of several combinations presenting similar entertainments, can their partial failure be accounted for.

The troupe left the city with nearly empty pockets, and in Colorado illness caused a cancellation of performances. Broke, the company dissolved, but Edouin and his wife chaperoned the young actress home.

In October 1881 she was back playing at New York's Bijou Opera House, a somewhat seasoned twenty-year-old performer who had no trouble in performance but had not yet learned the business side of the entertainment business. She'd seen how easily the money disappeared despite good reviews and a strong company. Fresh from the financial disaster in the West, her inexperience in the trade led her astray. Faced with a number of offers upon her return to New York, she found she could not say no.

Early in 1882 she signed conflicting contracts with rival companies and, threatened with litigation when all was revealed, escaped by sailing for England. While the press at home called her reckless and unsavory, her debut at London's Gaiety Theatre set her star ablaze.

Once again, her romantic inclinations betrayed her. She and Braham had divorced after the death of their baby, but she still had a soft spot for the boys in the band. In May 1884 she married, and again it was to a musician, English composer Edward Solomon. By the winter of the following year, Lillian, her husband, and their baby daughter, Dorothy, had returned to New York.

Reality slapped the face of the famous beauty once more. In England a woman named Jane Isaacs Solomon filed suit against her husband—for bigamy. Edward was arrested in England, and Lillian's hopes for a happy married life were shattered. She announced she would seek an annulment. Although she concealed the pain of Solomon's betrayal, the gorgeous petals of America's Beauty were tarnished by scandal. Even scandal, however, brought people to a theater.

Lillian decided to make another tour of the American West, and this one turned out to be much more successful. She signed with the J. C. Duff Company and embarked on a long tour of cities along the Pacific Coast. At the end of two seasons on the road, Lillian was a bigger star than ever. And, as she entered her thirties, she, herself, was bigger than ever. The hourglass figure that had contributed to her fame now required the tight cinching of a strong corset. Lillian, who reportedly could eat a dozen ears of corn as an appetizer, fully enjoyed the offerings of the best restaurants. Knowing her beauty was a huge part of her success, she began to exercise religiously. She became a fanatical bicyclist, and her friend, millionaire railroad salesman Diamond Jim Brady, presented her with a gold-plated bicycle.

Always questioned about her beauty secrets, Lillian recommended vigorous exercise at a time when the myth of women as the "weaker sex" was accepted without question. Lillian's advice flew in the face of convention. "Bicycle riding to women usually means peddling along dismounting every five or ten minutes, but this will not do at all if you mean to reduce your weight," she warned. In addition, and to the horror of those who already considered bicycles for women a tool of the devil, Lillian advised against wearing a corset while exercising. Every muscle must be unhampered, she insisted.

She also loosened the corset when she sat down to a feast with Diamond Jim. The legendary railroad equipment salesman had made, and spent, millions of dollars, and a lot of his profits went into huge dinner parties for himself and his friends. Lillian reportedly matched him at the table but handily outdid him at maintaining her weight. She once took off nearly thirty pounds and reduced her waist from 27 to 22 inches by sticking to a schedule of exercise that included bicycle riding, tennis, workouts in a gymnasium, Turkish baths, and massage.

In 1907 she was once again on tour in her private Pullman car. Her play, *Wildfire*, was a huge success. According to an enthusiastic report in the *Anaconda (Montana) Standard:*

Miss Lillian Russell, the celebrated actress and American beauty, is making her first visit to Butte. Miss Russell's public interviews and writings have long been noted for the good advice to young women, based on her own extended and varied experiences and observations.

Lillian's recommendations about religion were quoted extensively. "I am to a certain extent a believer in Christian Science. Mrs. [Mary Baker] Eddy's teachings are not new, however. Much of her arguments were taken from the Confessions of Marcus Aurelius. She has read Buddha, and dipped into the writings of Confucius. Her doctrines contain the best teachings of those ancient wise men," Lillian expounded, somewhat to the surprise of the *Standard* interviewer.

Marriage and divorce were also covered, with the star using the newspaper to advance some rather radical ideas for the time. "Marriage is not an ideal institution as it is," she said. "The idea that as soon as a man marries you that he should assume the airs of a proprietor and tell a woman where she should go and whom she should meet and why, especially if she is a woman of feeling, is irksome."

Irksome was too mild a word for Lillian's third marriage. In 1894 she wed a singer, John Haley Augustin Chatterton, who styled himself Signor Giovanni Perugini. Her actress friend Marie Dressler portrayed the tenor as a conceited buffoon who stooped to embarrassing Lillian onstage. After several months of discord, Lillian kicked him out. Disillusioned, she threw herself into her career, taking a hand in management of her company. Although her appearance in *The Goddess of Truth* and other productions under the direction of Henry E. Abby were not well received, she made a comeback in *An American Beauty* and thus acquired her nickname.

In 1899 Lillian joined Weber and Fields Music Hall, where she earned more than $1,200 a week. Until 1904, when Joe Weber and Lew Fields dissolved their partnership, she enjoyed a fizzy success in comic opera. *Lady Teazle,* a musical version of *The School for Scandal,* showcased her talents as an actress. Minor surgery on her throat had not helped her deteriorating voice, so she began playing exclusively comic roles. She covered thousands of miles in her private railroad car to indifferent success and finally returned to vaudeville and a popular reprise of some of her most famous songs.

Still beautiful, fiercely intelligent, as opinionated as her mother ever had been, Lillian began writing a syndicated newspaper column, lectured on health and beauty and love, supported the vote for women, and put out a line of cosmetics called Lillian Russell's Own Preparation.

In 1912 she married Alexander Pollock Moore, owner of the *Pittsburgh Leader*. Moore was everything her musician husbands had not been, and his power in conservative politics matched her interests well. She recruited for the Marine Corps and supported War Bond drives during the First World War and afterward raised money for the American Legion.

She made a movie version of *Wildfire* in 1914, starring with John Barrymore, but the movie was not particularly successful. Her public appearances, however, especially when she closed with her theme song, "Come Down My Evenin' Star," still roused huge enthusiasm. Her profile, which was as well known as her name, was featured on cigar bands and matchbox covers, theater posters, and magazine covers. The *Illustrated American* declared:

> There are those of course, who have preferences in other directions when it comes to female beauty. They may prefer theirs darker, or slighter, or more willowy, or shorter or taller. But any such predilection is a personal matter, after all, everyone acknowledges Miss Russell a beauty and a rare one at that.

Lillian always knew her beauty was an asset, but after her work for equal rights for women, for political causes, and on behalf of American servicemen, she decided to enter the political arena herself, and, so, in 1915, she declared her candidacy for mayor of New York. The woman whose first tour of the West had ended in economic failure had learned a lot about the world of commerce, and her candidacy was founded on the principles of sound business practice. "The reason I want to vote is because I pay three kinds of taxes—on my property, my income and my business—and I think I ought to have something to say about what to do with my money," she told the *New York Herald*.

Women did not receive the national right to vote until 1920, and Lillian's run for mayor did not succeed, except that it gave her another avenue to express the strong beliefs she had in equal rights. Despite her age her good looks still engaged the largely male press. One editor noted that if perennial beauty is an outward manifestation of inward spiritual grace, then New York's government should be crowned with success under her hand.

She campaigned vigorously for Warren G. Harding for president; as a result, in 1922 President Harding appointed her as a special investigator on immigration. During a tour of Europe in this capacity, she sustained a bad fall and, despite the injuries, turned in her report urging restrictions on immigration. Shortly after she'd completed her mission, the famous American Beauty, the superstar of the "Gay Nineties," died at her Pittsburgh home of "cardiac exhaustion."

Sarah Kirby Stark

PIONEER MANAGER

Ye that would have obedient wives, Beware of meddling woman's kind, officious counsel.

—John Hambleton to the *Evening Picayune*, San Francisco, January 1851

Sarah Kirby threw down the newspaper and paced across the room, only to turn and race back to the crumpled pages. She picked them up, smoothed them out, and once again read the diatribe against her penned by John Hambleton. Sarah was stricken with grief at the suicide of Hambleton's wife. That the actor should blame *her* for his wife's untimely death and publish his accusations in the San Francisco newspapers increased her distress. Her fingers whitened, and the edges of the page crumpled as she saw herself likened to a snake squeezing the life from its victim.

Hambleton wrote of his dead wife's devotion:

> For six years of struggling hardship through poverty and sickness she was at my side night and day, with the same watchful attention as a mother to an infant, until, with the last two months a change had taken place, like a black cloud over shadowing the bright sun. She gradually lost all affection for me, riveting her attention on a female friend who, like a fascinating serpent, attracted her prey until within her coils. In silence I observed this at first, and deemed it trifling, until I saw the plot thicken.

SARAH KIRBY STARK d. 1898

Sarah crushed the flimsy copy of the *Evening Picayune* again. She must counter this ugly story or lose her reputation in the city. Not for this had she struggled to attain a pinnacle of success as both an actress and a theater manager. As manager of a company of actors—one of very few women managers—bad publicity could cost her everything.

A genuine pioneer of theater in California, Sarah Kirby had made her debut in Boston but arrived in the brawling new territory within a year of the first rush of argonauts heading for the sparkling, gold-laced streams of the Sierra. Rowe's Amphitheater in San Francisco saw her first performance as Pauline in *The Lady of Lyons*. Two months later she appeared at the Tehama Theater, which she had opened and comanaged, in Sacramento. By August 1850 she was a full-fledged manager, producing plays at a theater in Stockton, and in September she was back at the Tehama in Sacramento.

Sarah was the widow of J. Hudson Kirby, also an actor. Sarah's debut on February 21, 1850, was under her stage name, Mrs. J. Hudson Kirby. Although she performed under the name Mrs. Kirby, she was during that time married to Jacob Wingard, who died shortly thereafter in San Francisco following a fall from a horse.

The events of January 1851 threatened everything she had built in the past year. Sarah recognized the precarious position she was in after the suicide of Mrs. Hambleton and the ravings of John Hambleton in the newspapers. The Hambletons had been popular on the stage from the time of their arrival from Australia, and John Hambleton was considered one of the best comedians in the city. If readers believed Hambleton's newspaper articles, public sentiment could likely turn against Sarah, so she decided to set the record straight. Her account of the tragedy was published in the San Francisco *Alta California* on January 16, 1851, the day after Hambleton's letter appeared in the *Picayune* and two days after the death of her friend:

Mrs. Hambleton made me her confidante, and in her state-
ments to me at that time she represented that her husband
treated her unkindly, harshly, and by acts and language abused
her to a cruel extent. About one month ago she stated to me
that she had been cruelly beaten by her husband, and showed
me the marks of violence upon her neck, where the marks of
her husband's fingers were made when he nearly choked her
to death; the skin was removed by the nails of his fingers as
she extricated herself from his grasp; her head was much
bruised, as she stated, from him knocking her down; and if
Mrs. Smith, the landlady, had not taken him off he would
have killed her.

Theater people often lived as dramatically as the plays they appeared in, and
while some notoriety might help fill the house, Sarah knew too much infamy could
turn the public away from even the best plays presented by the finest performers.
Despite the harrowing tale she'd been told and the physical evidence of abuse,
Sarah's newspaper account of the events said Sarah had advised Mrs. Hambleton to
return to her husband.

Other newspapers contributed another angle to the tale. Having appeared frequently onstage with the very popular Hambletons, Henry Coad had apparently
formed a close friendship with the battered Mrs. Hambleton. The *Alta California* first
mentioned Coad in the story that explained why the Jenny Lind Theater had been
dark on the evening of January 14. The newspaper announced that the "favorite
actress," Mrs. Hambleton, had committed suicide by drinking poison at her resi-
dence. Details were supplied in the story that followed:

It appears that the alliance between Mr. and Mrs.
Hambleton was not of a happy character, and that the latter
had conceived an ardent attachment to a member of the
company, Mr. Coad, who returned it with equal ardor. They

had, however, determined from prudential reasons to refrain from meeting each other or conversing until some opportunity should occur when they could unite their destinies.

The uneasy situation had continued for some days, the newspaper reported, until Mr. Hambleton jealously accused his wife of betraying her vows. If she would tell him who it was, Hambleton reportedly had assured his wife that he would consent to a separation so that she and her lover could go their own way. Apparently believing this, she told him it was Coad, who was called to their rooms at The Bell, a rooming house where all three lived. There, Hambleton threatened to blow out his rival's brains or kill them both unless Coad departed immediately. The young man did so.

Sarah knew the agonies that the third party in this triangle was suffering. If she had advised her friend to flee with the young actor who had befriended her, would that have prevented the tragedy or only led the jealous husband to commit greater harm?

The newspaper account related:

> Mrs. H., probably under the impression that [Coad] had deserted her, and been trifling with her affections merely, immediately swallowed a very large dose of some powerful corrosive poison. Medical aid was sent for as soon as it was discovered, but in about ten minutes she died. As soon as the fact that the object of his affections had poisoned herself was made known to Coad, he purchased a quantity of what he supposed was the same kind of compound, and attempted to poison himself. An emetic was administered soon after, and at last accounts he was doing well, although suffering severely.

The funeral cortege had barely passed the doors of the Parker House and the darkened Jenny Lind Theater before a new bombshell hit the papers. John Hambleton's accusation against Sarah Kirby was printed in the *Evening Picayune,* complete with details of his wife's terrible death, his actions, and a final finger pointing at the woman he blamed for the whole thing:

> I therefore, from my heart, attribute the cause of insanity to
> the evil counsels of Mrs. Kirby, and forgive the young man
> Coad, whose every action I have most acutely, though silently
> watched; for he was a victim as well as my poor wife.

Sarah could not let that indictment stand. Many people would not read between the lines and understand that Hambleton's obsessive watching of his wife's every move was as diabolically inclined as it had been, nor would they understand that his poor wife had suffered the violence that Hambleton had not meted out to Coad. If Sarah Kirby were to retain her standing, and her lease on the Jenny Lind, she would have to convince the world that she was not to blame.

Sarah recognized that even in rambunctious California, a serious actress and theater manager absolutely had to exhibit an exceptional character or risk alienating theater patrons. Rip-roaring Frisco was taking steps toward a more civilized image. The editor of the *Golden Era* magazine offered a blunt warning about the danger of corruption from the stage. He uncompromisingly suggested that "all persons of the theatrical profession" should have to provide a certificate of good character before being allowed to perform before the public.

In the short amount of time she'd spent in the area, Sarah had acquired a reputation for hard work and for providing the best theater fare in the city. This was reflected in an opinion in the *Alta California:*

> Since she has been with us in this city, she has spared neither
> time, labor nor expense in presenting for the public a series
> of dramatical entertainments characterized by discriminat-
> ing taste and sterling ability.

Sarah's skill as an actress was the cornerstone for the theater company she created. As manager, Sarah made all the decisions: She hired and paid for the theater, designed sets, chose costumes, and selected actors. The problems of her actors became her own. Her "good character" at a time women in the theater were often considered one step up from prostitutes was essential to her success—as well as the paychecks and reputations of those in her troupe.

California took its theater seriously, according to witnesses like Frank Marryat, an Englishman who traveled extensively and wrote of his adventures. "Perhaps in no other community so limited could one find so many well-informed and clever men—men of all nations, who have added the advantages of traveling to natural abilities and a liberal education," Marryat wrote of the gold miners arriving by the thousands from all over the world. There was a level of sophistication and unexpectedly puritan point of view when it came to serious drama that threatened Sarah and her company of actors.

But late in the week of the tragedy, other witnesses told their stories to the press, corroborating Sarah's version of the events that had ended in death for her friend and near death for another fine actor in her company.

The true test of public reaction to the scandal occurred a few days later, when Sarah appeared at the Jenny Lind. Tension among the troupe was high. No one could predict what would happen when the curtain rose. The *Alta California* reported that friends of Mr. Hambleton were expected to create such a disturbance that Sarah Kirby would be unable to perform:

> The theatre was filled soon after the doors were open, and upon the appearance of Mrs. Kirby in the character of Florinda in *The Apostate*, she was received in the most generous and hearty manner.

An attempt by half a dozen people to hiss and boo the actress was quelled soon after it began. Following the final act, the same newspaper reported that the audience rewarded her with applause

> long and deep and unanimous. She made a few appropriate remarks, which coming from her heart, found a channel to the hearts of the audience, and when she retired [for the evening] she received a regular storm of cheers. This was right, and we have now a higher respect for the American heart than we had before, if that is possible.

The newspaper also pointed out that the scandal had threatened the viability of the troupe. The loss of three performers meant that two other women in the company had to play men's parts. The performance, however, passed the test of San Francisco's theater critics and the public.

Having confirmed her respectability, Sarah continued to produce plays and present her customary roles. She appeared in a number of Shakespeare's most popular plays and acted in the light comedy that often completed an evening's entertainment.

Back in Sacramento that spring, Sarah opened the Tehama Theater for a benefit for local fire companies, all manned by unpaid volunteers. The *Sacramento Daily Union* praised theater managers James Stark and Sarah Kirby:

> We have never known the managers of a theatre exhibit a greater disposition to contribute to the advancement of charitable objects, or those measures which in our city cannot be sustained except by private donation.

She and the leading man in her troupe were married in June 1851 in Sacramento. Sarah and James Stark, a handsome man with an established reputation as an actor, completed their theatrical engagement on the evening of their wedding, then took a "matrimonial tour" to Marysville, a major center for miners headed for the gold-laced foothills some 30 miles away. James was described by fellow actor Walter Leman as "an admirable actor . . . a man of kind and generous feelings."

Sarah's newest husband, her third, had come to San Francisco late in 1850 and immediately established a reputation as a fine Shakespearean actor. James was especially successful with his role in *King Lear*, which was frequently lauded in newspapers. As a couple, Sarah Kirby Stark and James Stark were also recognized as "the first to render the theatre in California an institution worthy of the support of an intellectual and refined public."

As an accomplished performer, Sarah played tragedy and comedy with equal expertise. She was praised in the *Alta California* for her contributions to theater in her first years in California.

> She is our pioneer actress, and for the three years during which California has sprung almost from a wilderness to a proud State, she has labored incessantly to raise the drama to its present position among us.

Still she was careful of her reputation. In 1852, more than a year after the Hambleton affair that had so tested her courage, she played a man's role in *The Iron Chest*. A woman in trousers almost guaranteed a full house, yet Sarah was not comfortable, and some laughter from the front rows threw her off stride. At the conclusion of the play, her husband appeared and apologized for an uneven performance, caused, he said, "by the novelty of her dress." According to the *San Francisco Herald*:

> The audience immediately responded with hearty denials and chanted for the appearance of Sarah, who, when the tumult subsided, explained that necessity alone had induced her to take the part and wear the infamous trousers, there being no male actor available.

Over the next decade and more, Sarah continued to perform in theaters throughout California and in other western states. Sometimes she and her husband appeared together; sometimes they played roles in separate venues in disparate locations.

In Shakespeare's last, great tragedy, *Richard III*, both James and Sarah were recognized for their skills after a performance in Nevada City in 1857. According to a critic in the *Nevada Journal:*

> Mrs. Stark, it is superfluous to say, rendered most thrillingly
> the character of the Duchess of York—one so difficult that
> Shakespeare has often doubted if such a character could
> have existed in life.

Sarah returned to San Francisco several times, always bringing plays the public and critics applauded. Her company was praised by newspapers for the quality of the players, the dramas and comedies that were staged, and for the respectable lifestyle of its manager. Part of that was attributable to the benefits that she held to raise money for things like a hospital and churches. James, however, found the lure of the gold mines irresistible. He made a comfortable income as a miner, and when he died he left behind a quartz mill bearing his name in the remote canyon between Aurora and Bodie, now a well-preserved ghost town maintained by the California state park system

Once again she was a widow, but James Stark's success at gold mining left Sarah comfortably well off. All was not well, however. According to a lawsuit, Sarah was soon victimized in a property transaction. The property Sarah reportedly conveyed to her niece and husband carried a condition that they care for the aging actress as a member of the family. The *San Francisco Call* published a story in 1883 that detailed an action Sarah filed to recover title to the home on the corner of Twenty-fourth Street and San Jose Avenue. The report says that for many years Sarah had been an invalid, dependent upon the $75 monthly rent from the house. She had, reported the newspaper, "on two different occasions dislocated her hip, which has rendered her weak in body and mind, dependent and lonely and greatly in need of a home, kind care, and attention and society such as only relatives can bestow." The relatives in question apparently consigned her to a back room, and, when she felt compelled to leave, she was told never to return, even to remove her belongings.

She may have been "lonely" in May when the property changed hands, but by September she was married again, to another actor, Charles Thorne, whom she had initially met years before. According to old newspapers, the two veterans toured Australia and the Orient, and "did a good business."

Sarah died in December 1898. She had returned to San Francisco after Thorne's death, and the *San Francisco Chronicle* published a short piece noting that she was "a woman well known here in the early days as an actress of considerable ability."

Afterword

Without a witness human experience is an isolated exercise that enriches only a single soul at a time. Storytelling has been a necessary component of human life probably from the invention of language. We tell stories of our experiences every day, sharing the joke or the tragedy with others and expressing our thoughts and our dreams. Great storytellers are recognized in every civilization dating far back into the past.

Early settlers in the West were hungry for entertainment and often set up acting companies from among the available ranks, be they sailors rounding Cape Horn or gold miners camped under towering pines. Everything from Shakespearean drama to topical farce was performed for the entertainment of actors and audience alike. Men played the parts of women until actresses appeared on the western scene, and the addition of the ladies increased the audiences.

Life for an actress was risky, but it provided one of the earliest and most remunerative of professions for women. Many became managers, and a few became playwrights. Even then, a star system rewarded the best actresses with fame and fortune, but the biggest stars could flame out within a year and never be heard of again.

It was a life of hard work and adventure. A newspaper article recounting the experience of an actress determined to make a fortune in the gold-laced hills of California deals humorously with "barnstorming," so called because players often performed in any structure that could hold an audience. "There is a wild fascination in it that the well-paid actors in their palace cars never dream of," wrote the anonymous actress in 1889.

Determined to bring her talents to the isolated town of Bodie, now a state historic park, the actress scrounged up $50 from her friends, and found companions to form a partnership. They left San Francisco for Stockton on a steamer that charged 25 cents for passage, 50 cents for a berth and another 50 cents for dinner. The five-member troupe paid out their fares, intending to catch a train from Stockton and go on to Oakdale by stage, where they hoped to provide entertainment and recoup their fortunes. But the boat was late and the train was gone.

"Horrors upon horrors! To us the delay meant a sad regret, a return home, and, to me, a debtor to my friends. What did I do? I prayed. You smile. You think an actress cannot pray. No minister of the Gospel ever offered up a more fervent petition to God than I when kneeling in that little stateroom." Her prayers were answered when a local hotel owner listened to her woebegone tale and offered rooms and a meal. The next night they repaid their host by entertaining the local citizens. He recouped his costs at the bar.

So they went up into the mountains, carrying with them a large roll of donated canvas painted with the heads of presidents. They cut off George Washington to pay for accommodations in one place and played banjo, sang, danced, and performed a scene from *Hamlet* in another as they made their way ever upward toward the barren mountaintop. Two more presidents were lopped off to pay their way in Sonora. Within two days of their destination, with snow on the ground and a bitter wind blowing, they were refused a place to sleep at an isolated farm because "we don't want any show people here."

The last of their money paid for cots in the barn and cow shed, where a clear view of the full moon was revealed through the holes in the roof. The next morning they were served a breakfast of "black coffee and blacker bread," but they went on their way "rejoicing." In rip-roaring Bodie they played a week, restoring their fortunes. The actress, however, admitted "that was my last barnstorming tour."

A pretty face could help an actress, but talent earned her fame. The players in *Gilded Girls* all had more than just a pretty face and an ability to memorize lines. They had courage, intelligence, talent, and the will to succeed at a time when women were widely believed to be "the weaker sex." Their stories add to the richness of our past.

Bibliography

GENERAL SOURCES

Argonaut, 16 June 1877, 7 March 1898.

Auster, Albert. *Actresses and Suffragists*. New York: Praeger Publishers, 1984.

Belasco, David, and Dave Basso, eds. *Gala Days of Piper's Opera House and the California Theater*, 1919.

The Californian, 4 November 1848.

Chinoy, Helen Krich, Jenkins, and Linda Walsh, eds. *Women in American Theatre*. New York: Theatre Communications Group, Inc., 1987.

Gagey, Edmond M. *The San Francisco Stage, A History*. New York: Columbia University Press, 1950.

Furman, Evelyn E. Livingston. *The Tabor Opera House, A Captivating History*. Colorado: Self-published, 1972. Library of Congress Catalogue Number 72-88027

James, Edward T., Janet Wilson James, and Paul S. Boyer, eds. *Notable American Women 1607–1950*. Cambridge, Mass: Belknap Press of Harvard Univ. Press, 1971.

Leman, Walter M. *Memories of an Old Actor*. San Francisco: A. Roman Co., Publishers, 1886.

MacMinn, George R. *The Theater of the Golden Era in California*. Caldwell, Idaho: Caxton Printers, Ltd., 1941.

Marryat, Frank. *Mountains and Molehills: Recollections of a Burnt Journal*. New York: J.B. Lippincott Company, 1855.

Robinson, Alice M., Vera Mowry Roberts, and Milly S. Barranger, eds. *Notable Women in the American Theatre, A Biographical Dictionary*. New York: Greenwood Press, 1989.

Rourke, Constance. *Troupers of the Gold Coast*. New York: Crowell Publishing Co., 1928.

Smith, Sean W. *A Woman's Role: Gender and the Legitimate Theater in Gold Rush San Francisco, 1848–1856*. Ann Arbor: UMI Company, 1999.

MAUDE ADAMS

Davies, Actor. *Maude Adams*. Denver, Colo.; Frederick A. Stokes Co., 1901.

Robins, Phyllis. *Maude Adams: An Intimate Portrait*. New York: D. Appleton, 1956.

———. *The Young Maude Adams*. New York: D. Appleton, 1959.

Seagraves, Anne. *Women Who Charmed the West*. Lakeport, Calif.: Wesanne Publications, 1991.

"Women in American History." *Encyclopedia Britannica* Web site. www.britannica.com.

MARY ANDERSON

Anderson, Mary. *A Few Memories*. London: Osgood, McIlvaine & Co, 1896.

———. *A Few More Memories*. London: Hutchinson & Co, 1936.

Daily Alta California, 4-16 April, 20-27 August 1876; 5, 27 August 1886.

Farrar, J. M. *Mary Anderson, The Story of Her Life and Professional Career.* London: David Bogue, 1884.

The Grizzly Bear, September 1907.

Oakland Tribune, 9 June 1940.

Sacramento Bee, 29 May 1940.

Sacramento Union, 3 April 1886.

San Francisco Call, 19 May 1891.

San Francisco Chronicle, 27 February, 1 April 1903; 22 May 1921.

SARAH BERNHARDT

American Heritage, July/August 1989.

Anaconda Standard, 23–27 September 1891; 25 April, 6 May 1906.

Argonaut, 21 May 1881, 4 January 1897.

Bernhardt, Sarah. *The Art of the Theatre.* New York: Books for Libraries Press, reprint 1969.

———— *Memories of My Life.* New York: D. Appleton, 1907.

Butte Miner, 27 February 1921.

Izard, Forrest. *Sarah Bernhardt, An Appreciation.* New York: Sturgis & Walton Company, 1915.

Montana Standard, 27 March 1903, 7 May 1978.

New Theatre Quarterly, February 1994.

San Francisco Call, 10, 16, 17 May 1887; 14, 25 April, 6 September 1891.

Seattle Post-Intelligencer, 24, 25 September 1891.

Skinner, Cornelia Otis. *Madame Sarah.* Boston: Houghton Mifflin Company, 1967.

Smithsonian, August 2001.

Theatre Magazine, 1906.

Theatre Research International, Spring 1993.

The (San Francisco) Wave, 2 May 1891.

MRS. LESLIE CARTER

Argonaut, August 1897.

Belasco, David. *The Theatre Through Its Stage Door.* New York: Harper and Brothers Publishers, 1919.

Liberty Magazine, 15 January–19 March 1927.

New York Times, 14 November 1937.

San Francisco Call, 10 February 1889.

San Francisco Chronicle, 7 December 1902; 5, 14 June 1904.

Sunset Magazine, July 1904.

Timberlake, Craig. *The Bishop of Broadway, The Life and Work of David Belasco.* New York: Library Publishers Inc., 1954.

CAROLINE CHAPMAN

A History of Tuolumne County, California. San Francisco: B. F. Alley, 1882.

Daily Alta California, 24 May, 10, 29 June, 7 December 1853; 1 January 1862; 9, 13 May 1876; 3 March 1980.

Gold Hill News, 15 May, 28 September 1865; 6 April 1871.

Golden Era, 26 June 1853.

Nevada Journal, 22 November, 11–25 December 1851.

Placer Times, 30 March, 1–20 May 1850.

Sacramento Times and Transcript, 9, 19, 21, 25 May, 1, 18 June 1850; 25 December 1851.

Sacramento Union, 8, 28–31 May, 4–14 June 1851; 19 November 1972.

San Francisco Call, 30 November 1862; 10 October, 5 December 1887.

San Francisco Herald, 20 June 1854, 27 March 1857, 3 April 1859.

San Francisco Examiner, 16 July 1928.

CATHERINE HAYES

Ahlquist, Karen. *Democracy at the Opera.* New York: New York Press, 1997.

O'Mara, Joseph. *If These Walls Could Talk.* Limerick, Ireland: Limerick Press, 1972.

Preston, Katherine K. *Opera on the Road: Traveling Troupes in the US, 1825–1860.* Chicago: University of Illinois Press, 1995.

Van der Pas, Peter W. "Kate Hayes." *Nevada County Historical Society Bulletin,* Vol. 42, No. 1, January 1988.

Walsh, Basil. *Catherine Hayes: The Hibernian Prima Donna.* Dublin, Ireland, and Portland, Ore.: Irish Academic Press, 2000.

MATILDA HERON

Browne, Ross J. Review of Miss Heron's performance. *Territorial Enterprise,* Virginia City, Nevada, 17 April 1866.

James, Edward T., Janet Wilson James, and Paul S. Boyer, eds. *Notable American Women 1607–1950.* Cambridge, Mass.: Belknap Press of Harvard University Press, 1971.

Johnson, Allen, and Malone Dumas. *Dictionary of American Biography.* New York: Charles Scribner's Sons, 1931.

McCabe, John H. *The Theatre of the Golden Era in California.* San Francisco: San Francisco Press, 1910.

Soule, Frank. Various articles. *California Chronicle,* January 1854.

Wilson, James G., and John Fiske. *Encyclopedia of America Biography.* New York: D. Appleton, 1888.

LILLIE LANGTRY

Allardyce, Nicoll. *A History of English Drama.* Boston: Cambridge University Press, 1967.

Bodley, John E. *Mr. Gladstone Prepares to Meet Mrs. Langtry.* New York: Brooks Publishing, 1925.

Brough, James. *The Prince and the Lily.* London: Coward Press, 1954.

"The Jersey Lily as a Later Helen of Troy." *The Literary Digest,* March 1929.

Langtry, Lillie. *The Days I Knew.* London: Futura Publications, 1925.

Plimpton, Margaret. *The Life and Loves of Lillie Langtry.* London: Dumont, 1931.

Seagraves, Anne. *Women Who Charmed the West.* Lakeport, CA: Wesanne Publications, 1991.

"Thespians in Arcady." *The Island Magazine,* No. 6, 8 September 1819.

ADAH MENKEN

Davis, Sam. "The History of Nevada." *Nevada Monthly,* Vol. 2, July 1880.

Gosse, Edmund. "The Life of Algernon Charles Swinburne." *Dictionary of National Biography.* 1917.

James, Edwin. *Biography of Adah Isaacs Menken.* New York: New York Press, 1881.

Mankowitz, Wolf. *Mazeppa, the Lives, Loves, and Legends of Adah Isaacs Menken.* New York: Stein and Day Publishers, 1982.

Rourke, Constance. *Troupers of the Old Gold Coast.* New York: New York Press, 1928.

Stoddard, Charles W. "La Belle Menken." *National Magazine,* Boston, Mass. February 1905.

HELENA MODJESKA

Daily Alta California, 21, 26 August 1877.

Daily Nevada State Journal, 31 October 1877.

Footlight, 23–26 October 1877.

Gronowicz, Antoni. *Modjeska, Her Life and Loves.* New York: Thomas Yoseloff, Inc., 1956.

Idaho Statesman, 21, 22 March 1901.

Modjeska, Helena. *Memories and Impressions.* New York: MacMillan, 1910.

Payne, Theodore. *Life on the Modjeska Ranch in the Gay Nineties.* Los Angeles: The Kruckeberg Press, 1962.

Reno Evening Gazette, 25, 29 October 1877.

San Francisco Call, 10 February 1889, 21 January 1906, 9 April 1909.

Territorial Enterprise, 23 October 1877.

Wingate, Charles E. *Shakespeare's Heroines on the Stage.* New York: Thomas Y. Crowell & Company, 1895.

LUCILLE MULHALL

"America's First Cowgirl." *Oklahoma Weekly,* Oklahoma City, Okla., November 2001.

"Famous Mulhall Family." *Philadelphia Evening Item,* Philadelphia, Pa., 6 September 1907.

Ketchum, Richard M. *Will Rogers, His Life and Times.* New York: American Heritage
    Publishing Co, Inc., 1973.

Olds, Fred. "The Story of Lucille." *The War Chief of the Indian Territorial Posses of Oklahoma
    Westerners,* Vol. 8, No. 3, December 1974.

Savage, Candace. *Born to be a Cowgirl.* Berkeley, Calif.: Tricycle Press, 2001.

Stansbury, Kathryn. *Lucille Mulhall Wild West Cowgirl.* Mulhall, Okla.: Homestead Heirlooms
    Publishing, 1985.

KATE ROCKWELL

Cain, Trudy. *The Belle of the Yukon.* Dawson, Alaska: Rasmunson Publishing, 1997.

Morgan, Murray C. *Alexander Pantages.* New York: The Viking Press, 1960.

"The Real Klondike Kate." *Northern Review.* Yukon College, Whitehorse, Yukon, Canada.
    No. 19, Winter 1998.

"Whatever Happened to Klondike Kate." *Alaska Today,* Spokane, Wash., December 1995.

"Women of the Klondike." *America's Past,* Fairbanks, Alaska, No. 1004, July 1979.

LILLIAN RUSSELL

Anaconda Standard, 26, 29 May 1907; 9, 12 May 1909.

Argonaut, 23, 30 April, 14 May 1881.

Auster, Albert. *Actresses and Suffragists.* New York: Praeger Publishers, 1984.

Burke, John. *Duet in Diamonds. The Flamboyant Saga of Lillian Russell and Diamond Jim Brady in
    America's Gilded Age.* New York: GP Putnam's Sons, 1972.

Cosmopolitan Magazine, February–September 1922.

Montana Standard, 7 May 1978.

San Francisco Call, 27 April, 8, 15, 22 May 1881.

Theatre Magazine, February 1905.

SARAH KIRBY STARK

Daily Alta California, 4 November 1850; 16, 19 January 1851; 19 June 1851.

Nevada Journal, 3, 10, 17, 24 August 1855; 19, 26, June, 3 July 1857; 26 June 1872.

Sacramento Union, 19 November 19 1972.

Sacramento Transcript, 30 May 30 1851.

San Francisco Call, 16 September, 20 October 1883.

San Francisco Chronicle, 10 December 1898.

San Francisco Daily Union, 29 May 1851.

San Francisco Evening Picayune, 16 January 1851.

Index

About the Authors

JoAnn Chartier

JoAnn Chartier is a broadcast journalist and talk show host living and working in California's Gold Country. Her writing has earned regional and national awards from professional associations.

Chris Enss

Chris Enss is an author and screenwriter who has had several scripts optioned and has won awards for her screenwriting, stage plays, and short subject films.

Chris Enss (left) and JoAnn Chartier

For more history of the Old West, the authors invite you to visit their Web site, www.gypsyfoot.com.